*In this year of the Silver Jubilee of Her Majesty The Queen, it is a happy coincidence that the railway here in the Eastern part of her realm is poised on the brink of a fresh chapter in passenger rail travel.*

*That new chapter – the Era of the High Speed Train – will bring the cities of Her Majesty's Kingdom even closer in time than they are today.*

*The past 25 years have brought changes to the railways of Britain that are now more sweeping and more significant than those of the previous century. For they have been witness to the last days and ultimate demise of the steam locomotive – revered but outmoded victim of time and circumstance – the emergence of the new forms of power, diesel and electric traction and now, as a natural step in British Rail's quest for improved journey times, the evolution of the High Speed Train.*

*The four-minute train mile of 1825 will become the 28-second mile when Inter-City 125 – the High Speed Train – is introduced into commercial service on the East Coast Main Line next year.*

*The birth of this streamlined thoroughbred is a story of British technological triumph derived from the lessons of history, the demands of today and tomorrow and an unshakeable faith in the future of railways as a prime carrier in this crowded island of ours.*

*The quest for speed on the East Coast Main Line is, like Macaulay's History of England a "history of progress". To tell that story in its fullness, from the birth of railways here in this corner of the realm to the exciting new era now confronting the rail traveller, three quite independent writers from widely divergent walks of life have contributed – one an established railway historian whose books on steam locomotives are among the best, the second an oil company executive who has become an enthusiastic chronicler of the modern railway, and the third a member of my own staff who shares with me, and all railwaymen, the conviction that the railway is an invaluable asset which has a major contribution to make to the future transport needs of this nation. I commend this story to you.*

*G. Myers.*

*Autumn 1977*

General Manager, Eastern Region

# EARLY PACE MAKERS

By

P. W. B. Semmens, M.A., C.Chem., F.R.I.C., M.B.C.S.,
Assistant Keeper, National Railway Museum

Although today we automatically associate railways with high speed travel, the initial impact of the steam locomotive was not primarily in the field of speed. When *"Locomotion"*, the remote ancestor of today's East Coast express locomotives, trundled its train from Shildon to Stockton in 1825, it was the vast load it handled, rather than its speed, that struck the more discerning onlooker. Four years later, however, the competition of the Rainhill Trials resulted in the steam locomotive reaching speeds of over 30 m.p.h., and from then onwards many of the speed records achieved with steam traction resulted similarly from competition of one sort or another.

An early form of railway rivalry was the "Battle of the Gauges" between those railways employing what we now know as the Standard Gauge (4 feet 8½ inches, or its metric equivalent of 1432mm) and those built to Brunel's Broad Gauge of 7 feet 0¼ inch (2140mm). The Gauge Commissioners set up by Parliament conducted extensive inquiries into the advantages of the two systems, and trials were carried out in 1845. For the Standard Gauge a special locomotive, known simply as "A" or the *"Great A"*, was built by Robert Stephenson & Co. This 2–4–0 achieved an average speed of nearly 48 m.p.h. between Darlington and York and later succeeded in reaching 60 m.p.h. Although this performance was inferior to that achieved by the Broad Gauge locomotive with which it was in competition, it nevertheless represented the start of the high-speed running for which this section of the East Coast Main Line was to become famous.

The year 1845 was also notable for some remarkable long-distance speed achievements following George Hudson's election as Member of Parliament for Sunderland. A special train carrying the results of the poll reached London in eight hours from Sunderland, and was back in the constituency the next morning with copies of "The Times" containing the results of the by-election before they had actually been officially declared at 11.00 a.m. At that time the route that trains had to follow was very different from the East Coast Main Line as we know it today, and the train used Euston as its London terminus.

It was not until 1848 that the East Coast Route was complete between London and Edinburgh, although even then some of the sections we use now had not been constructed, and various round-about lines were followed up to 1871 when the railway from Shaftholme to Chaloners Whin completed the route that we know today. Opening of the King Edward Bridge at Newcastle did not take place until 1906, so even in this century there were minor changes of route still occurring.

Development of the East Coast Main Line in this piecemeal way meant that the various successive sections could differ markedly in their suitability for high-speed running, and this legacy had its effect on locomotive performance right to the end of steam in the 1960s. Until 1923, trains between London and Edinburgh had to operate over the lines of three separate railway companies—the Great Northern, the North Eastern, and the North British—and disputes between the partners were not unknown. Indeed, as late as 1897 the North British suddenly terminated the agreement under which the main Anglo-Scottish expresses were worked through by North Eastern engines over North British metals north of Berwick, until the dispute was settled. As a

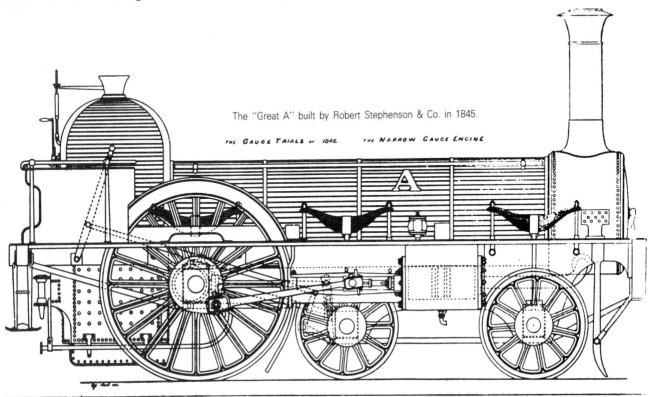

The "Great A" built by Robert Stephenson & Co. in 1845.

THE GAUGE TRIALS OF 1846      THE NARROW GAUGE ENGINE

## *Archibald Sturrock (1816-1909)*

Locomotive Engineer, G.N.R. 1850–1866

His No. 215 of 1853 would have been capable of running from King's Cross to Edinburgh in eight hours.

## *Edward Fletcher (1807-1889)*

Locomotive Superintendent, N.E.R. 1854–1882

Perhaps his best known locomotives were the 901 Class 2–4–0s, the principal express type used between York and Edinburgh from 1872 until the mid-1880s.

*Patrick Stirling (1820-1895)*

Locomotive Engineer, G.N.R. 1866–1895

The eight-foot bogie 4–2–2 designed by Stirling entered service in 1870, and for over 25 years this type worked East Coast trains between King's Cross and York.

*Thomas William Worsdell (1838-1916)*

Locomotive Superintendent, N.E.R. 1885–1890

With locomotives like his "D" Class 2–4–0s he laid the foundations of much needed standardisation in design.

*Wilson Worsdell (1850-1920)*

Locomotive Superintendent, N.E.R. 1890–1902
(redesignated) Chief Mechanical Engineer 1902–1910

In addition to building increasingly powerful 4–4–0s he designed the first 4–6–0 passenger locomotive to run on British metals in 1899.

*Henry Alfred Ivatt (1851-1923)*

Locomotive Engineer, G.N.R. 1896–1911

His major innovation was the introduction of the first 4–4–2 ''Atlantic'' type express passenger locomotive to run in Britain.

*Sir Vincent Litchfield Raven (1859-1934)*

Chief Mechanical Engineer, N.E.R. 1910–1922
Technical Adviser, L.N.E.R.' 1923–1924

His post-war scheme for electrifying the Main Line north of York was abandoned due to lack of money; his final steam locomotive design, the "City" Class "Pacifics" did not match the success of his "Z" Class "Atlantics".

*Sir (Herbert) Nigel Gresley (1876-1941)*

Locomotive Engineer, G.N.R. 1911–1922
Chief Mechanical Engineer, L.N.E.R. 1923–1941

Although responsible for many technical innovations, his crowning achievement was undoubtedly the A4 "Pacifics" which first appeared in 1935.

*Edward Thompson (1881-1954)*

Chief Mechanical Engineer, L.N.E.R. 1941–1946

Often criticised for changes in policy and design, necessitated by shortages of materials and lack of maintenance. However, his A2 "Pacifics" took their place in the East Coast Main Line fleet, until displaced by diesels in the 1960s.

*Arthur Henry Peppercorn (1889-1951)*

Chief Mechanical Engineer, L.N.E.R. 1946–1947
and British Railways E/N.E. Regions 1947–1949

Peppercorn added yet a further new "Pacific" type, the A1 (shown on the left in the photograph) to those already in use on the East Coast Main Line.

consequence the North British had to increase the running speeds on its section of line in order to cover the time lost changing engines at Berwick.

In spite of these early difficulties, there was a remarkable development in 1853 when a special locomotive was built for the Great Northern by R. W. Hawthorn. This was No. 215, a 4–2–2 with a large tender, and writing about it a decade later, Archibald Sturrock, the Railway's Locomotive Engineer, stated that it "could and did run 100-mile lengths at the highest present speeds. This locomotive was constructed to prove to the directors of the Great Northern Railway that it was quite practicable to reach Edinburgh from King's Cross in eight hours by only stopping at Grantham, York, Newcastle and Berwick." Unfortunately, there was at that time no commercial requirement for such speeds, as Sturrock remarked, "because there was no demand by travellers for, nor competition amongst, the railways to give the public such accommodation." Before the 19th Century was over, however, railway rivalry was to produce some very spectacular speed achievements on the East Coast Route.

The Great Northern main line south of Doncaster did not serve many major industrial centres, but that railway was able to utilise its line to provide competitive services for many West Riding towns and even as far west as Manchester and Liverpool. A study of the pre-1923 railway map of South-west Yorkshire shows Great Northern lines penetrating to many quite unlikely places (such as Halifax, Shipley and Keighley), but when these routes are viewed on the ground it is usually found that, to attain its objective, the Great Northern had to come over or through some of the most formidable hills. For instance, when today's diesels have laboured their way up from Leeds or Mirfield to Morley Tunnel, they are still well below the altitude of the now-abandoned G.N. line that ran from Wakefield to Bradford over the top via Tingley and Gildersome.

Not content with destinations that could be reached over their own metals, the Great Northern joined forces with the Manchester, Sheffield & Lincolnshire Railway in 1857 to operate their "Manchester Flyers" via Woodhead Tunnel. These trains were later to have better timings between Manchester and London than either the Midland or the London & North Western Railways with their easier or more direct routes. In order to achieve such competitive overall schedules, high speeds had to be maintained over the Great Northern main line south of Retford or Doncaster. In 1884 averages of over 53 m.p.h. were being scheduled for the Manchester trains between London and Grantham, and these speeds were probably the fastest in the world at that time.

## Racing to the North . . .

The biggest outburst of competition on the East Coast Route, however, was in the "Railway Races to the North" which took place on two occasions separated by a gap of seven years. The first "round" was in 1888, and followed the East Coast Route's decision to allow third-class passengers to use the "Special Scotch Express" between London and Edinburgh. This train, the 10.00 a.m. from King's Cross, was to become in time today's *Flying Scotsman*, and as running at the beginning of 1888 it took 9 hours for the 392.9 miles, although this schedule allowed time for a lunch stop. By the end of August when the Races finished, the East Coast Route had achieved an overall timing of 7 hours 27 minutes, in spite of the normal lunch stop at York, and with, in addition, a delay at Selby while a hay barge passed through the swing bridge. Although this was the fastest single journey over the route, the performance was consistently good during August. During the whole month, the times over the 82.7-mile stretch from Grantham to York only varied between 88 and 92 minutes, corresponding to average speeds of 53 to 56 m.p.h.

The Great Northern and North Eastern Railways had adopted rather different locomotive policies during the years preceding these Races, and their individual choices of engines for this

# GT. NORTHERN
### RAILWAY.

# PETERBORO
## OCTOBER.

IN ADDITION TO THE REGULAR

# EXCURSION
## TRAINS
### PASSENGERS FOR THE
# EXHIBITION

Will be conveyed daily (Sundays excepted) from Peterboro by the 7.0 a.m. Train, and Back by any Excursion Train. 1st and 2nd Class up to the 20th October, and 3rd Class Passengers up to the 18th October

## FARES, UNTIL FURTHER NOTICE.

 **6**s. |  **5**s. |  **3**s.

BY ORDER    SEYMOUR CLARKE, General Manager

An almost explosive growth in traffic began on the East Coast Route barely a year after the G.N.R. Main Line opened throughout. The basic cause was the Great Exhibition of 1851 when, for the first time, thousands who had hardly moved more than a few miles from home in their lives, flocked to the Capital to marvel at the wonders of the Crystal Palace. The poster, one of the earliest surviving examples of railway publicity, advertises some of the many extra trains which were required and the locomotive is one of the larger engines designed by Sturrock to cope with expanding traffic in the 1850s.

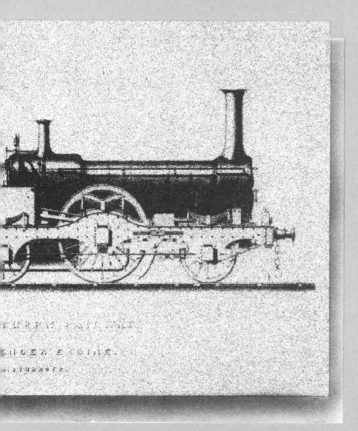

seen at Darlington North Road Station Museum.

The overall speeds achieved in these Races were not reached solely as a result of the provision of powerful locomotives. Equally as important had been the introduction of continuous automatic braking systems during the decade or so preceding the contest. There was, however, a lack of standardisation. While the North Eastern and North British had adopted the Westinghouse brake, the Great Northern, like most railways in Britain, had opted for the vacuum brake. Through coaches on East Coast expresses thus had to be fitted with both forms of equipment.

At the end of August 1888, the rival authorities got together and agreed not to cut their times between London and Edinburgh below 8¼ hours, and while the East Coast Route used such a timing from then onwards, the West Coast people, with their somewhat greater mileage between the two cities, eased their overall time to 8½ hours. This nevertheless represented an improvement of an hour-and-a-half on the best West Coast schedule before the racing began, although, since the East Coast running had originally been faster, their overall improvement was only three-quarters-of-an-hour. Even then, there were those who queried the necessity for such time savings, but there seems little doubt that the Races had given a welcome stimulus to railway engineering technology as a whole, so that, when the second "round" took place seven years later, the increase in speeds was remarkable.

The agreement between the East and West Coast Routes was for the overall London to Edinburgh schedules, and when the Forth Bridge was completed—in 1890—there was potentially another cause for rivalry. Before this, the East Coast Route had not been in contention for the fastest London to Aberdeen timings, with its passengers either having to take a ferry across the Firth of Forth or to travel via Stirling. After the bridge came into use, however, the distance between King's Cross and Aberdeen by the East Coast Route dropped to 523.2 miles, compared

high-speed running produced quite a contrast. The former company was responsible for the motive power between London and York, and changed engines at Grantham. Patrick Stirling's "Singles" were used throughout, and on the southern section the 2–2–2 variety alternated with the 4–2–2 type, as exemplified by No. 1, now preserved at the National Railway Museum in York. Between York and Edinburgh the North Eastern used four-coupled locomotives such as the Worsdell compound 4–4–0s and the Tennant 2–4–0s. The first of the latter class, No. 1463, is in the National Collection and can be

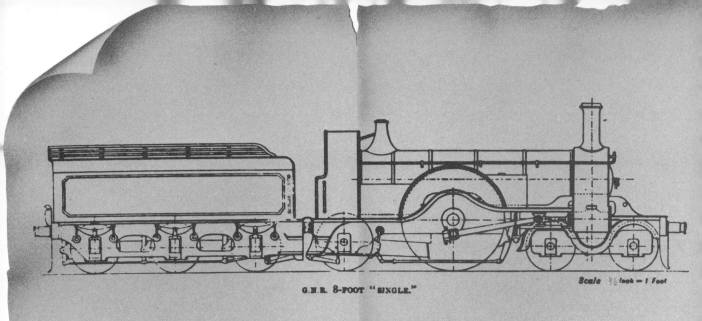

G.N.R. 8-FOOT "SINGLE."

Scale ⅛ inch = 1 Foot

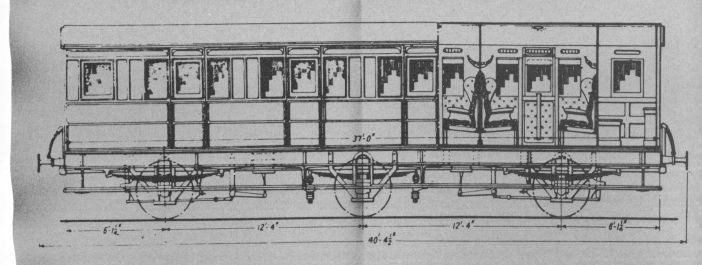

37'-0"

6'-1¼"     12'-4"     12'-4"     6'-1¼"

40'-4½"

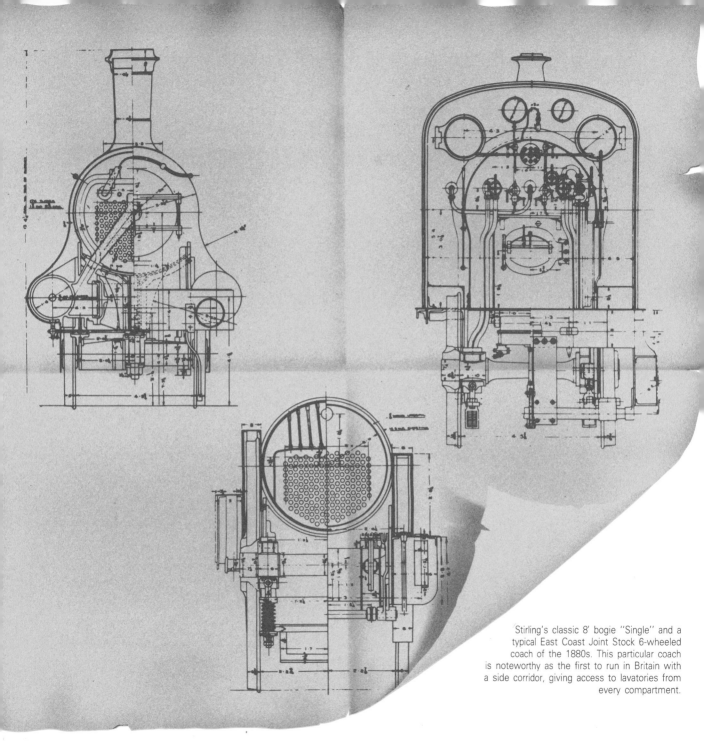

'Stirling's classic 8' bogie "Single" and a typical East Coast Joint Stock 6-wheeled coach of the 1880s. This particular coach is noteworthy as the first to run in Britain with a side corridor, giving access to lavatories from every compartment.

THE WORLDS MOST FAMOUS TRAIN

FLYING SCOTSMAN

1/-
FOURTH
EDITION

with the 539.7 miles via Crewe and Carlisle. The rivalries of 1888 had been suppressed but never extinguished and so it was only really a question of "when" rather than "if" the racing would begin all over again. It was mid-July 1895 when the starting flag dropped once more. In newspaper advertisements on 15 July the West Coast authorities announced that they would cut 40 minutes off the timing of their overnight express to Aberdeen, starting that very evening. They more than succeeded, and the train arrived 13 minutes early. However, while this initial acceleration was sprung on the East Coast Route as a surprise, their reaction was immediate.

In considering the events of the ensuing five weeks, the part played by the railway operating authorities must not be overlooked in the limelight that is inevitably concentrated on the locomotives. Like most of us today, railway officers are accustomed to pick up a telephone and have a direct conversation with their opposite number at the end of the line, but in 1895 the best communication system was the telegraph. Messages had to be written out, taken to the office and then transmitted, letter by letter, while at the receiving end the process had to be carried out in reverse. The ability of the rival routes to counter each other's achievements was thus a tribute equally to their administrative organisation and the hard work and skill of the locomotive crews.

The East Coast's point of view is best summarised by the letter from Patrick Stirling at Doncaster to the District Superintendent at Peterborough on 14 August. This started: "The L.& N.W. Company have expressed their intention to reach Aberdeen before us. This of course we cannot permit . . ." On the night of 21/22 August,

New coaches introduced in the 1928–1930 period, meant that passengers could while away the long non-stop journey on the "Flying Scotsman" by having their hair cut (top left). All the cooking (top right) was done by electricity. The Third Class accommodation (centre), although fairly Spartan, was comfortable; and the First Class Saloons (bottom) were designed to 'suggest a private dining room, decorated in 18th Century style'. The cover of the popular "Flying Scotsman" handbook (far left) published in 1931.

the East Coast Route succeeded in reaching Aberdeen 14 minutes ahead of their rivals in 520 minutes from King's Cross, and, with that, rested on their laurels, reverting to the published timetable rather than running ahead of time where they could.

The improvements in locomotive performance over the Races of 1888 was most marked, with trains achieving an overall average of more than a mile-a-minute over the whole distance, including various engine changes. To do this, the various sections had to be run flat out, and some remarkable performances resulted. Amongst the public, the nightly Race took on the nature of a sporting event, and crowds gathered at many of the intermediate stops to watch the locomotives being changed. At Newcastle, where the trains had to reverse in those days, one of the newspapers recorded: "amid enthusiastic cheers and waving of handkerchiefs the next stage of the journey was resumed."

Great risks were, however, taken at times and on one occasion, when the engine was North Eastern 4–4–0 No. 1621, now preserved at the National Railway Museum, the express went through Portobello station at over 80 m.p.h. in spite of the official limit at that time of only 15 m.p.h. One of the railway enthusiasts timing the train, on picking himself up from the floor, remarked: "We would have made bonnie raspberry jam in that Duddingston Road." There must have been relief all round, therefore, when the East Coast authorities reverted to published timings, even though the West Coast Route, the next night, racing solely against the clock, achieved a time of 512 minutes over the 539.7 miles, an overall average of 63.3 m.p.h. which was never beaten by steam. The star of that particular night was undoubtedly the L.N.W.R. 2–4–0 "Hardwicke", which can be seen today, preserved in full working order, at the National Railway Museum, standing next to some of her rivals of eighty years ago. In July 1896 the West Coast Scotch Express was derailed while passing through Preston at excessive

Steaming south from Newcastle is Britain's first streamlined train "The Silver Jubilee", hauled by A4 "Pacific" No. 4495 "Golden Fleece". And alongside, a Newcastle–Liverpool, via Sunderland, train hauled by A3 "Pacific" No. 2505 "Cameronian".

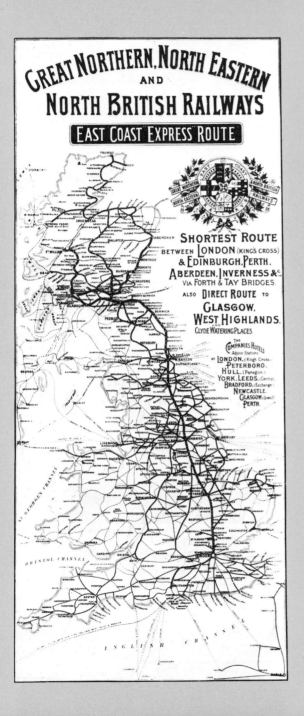

speed. This accident prevented any further competitive running for several years.

Clearly, the speeds achieved in the Races to Aberdeen were not to be attained regularly in ordinary service, but it was not long before the everyday averages started to creep upwards. In 1902 the North Eastern Railway introduced a timing of 43 minutes over the 44.1 miles between Darlington and York, and for nearly 21 years this remained the fastest scheduled run in the British Empire. Timings were eased during World War I, but the same schedule was reintroduced in 1922. The train concerned was not the same, however, and the new recipient of the title was a much heavier evening Glasgow–Leeds express instead of the relatively light Alnmouth–York train which had conveyed through coaches for the Midland.

In the 1890s, East Coast publicity was restrained, as this route poster shows. Nevertheless, by careful use of different thicknesses for lines, the impression is given that the West Coast Route does not exist. The ornate typography makes an interesting contrast with the route folder opposite, produced in the early 1970s. Also shown is a selection of named train booklets.

## Atlantics and Pacifics . . .

As coaching stock and trains generally
increased in weight during the early part of the 20th
Century, so motive power was improved. In 1898
the Great Northern had introduced the "Atlantic"
(4–4–2) wheel arrangement to Britain with No. 990
*"Henry Oakley"*, now preserved as part of the
National Collection and to be seen at work from
time to time on the Keighley & Worth Valley
Railway. Four years later Ivatt increased the power
capacity of the design by putting a larger boiler on
the same wheels and motion, the wide firebox being
spread out above the trailing wheels. After being
fitted with 32-element superheaters in later years,
their potential increased further and the engines
remained in express passenger service right down to
the start of World War II. The power which a
locomotive can produce is basically determined by
its ability to burn coal and the wide firebox
tradition was continued when, in 1922, the first of
the Gresley "Pacifics" was completed at Doncaster.

The first locomotive with the "Pacific" or
4–6–2 wheel arrangement to be built in Britain had
been *"The Great Bear"* which appeared on the
G.W.R. in 1908. While Churchward had
introduced many features that were to set new
standards of performance in this country, there
were various failings with *"The Bear"*, which was
rather too elongated to be satisfactory from an
operating viewpoint. In 1924 parts of it were rebuilt
as a "Castle" 4–6–0, by which time the first few
Gresley "Pacifics" were in service. In the British
Empire Exhibition at Wembley in 1924, the second
of these, by then named *"Flying Scotsman"*, was
exhibited alongside *"Pendennis Castle"* and
following this a series of Interchange Trials took
place between the two designs. Much to the
surprise of all those who were not acquainted with
the details of the Swindon design, the "Castles"
came out the better of the two, in spite of the
obviously larger dimensions of the Doncaster
engines.

It transpired that comparatively small
changes in the design of the valve gear were all that

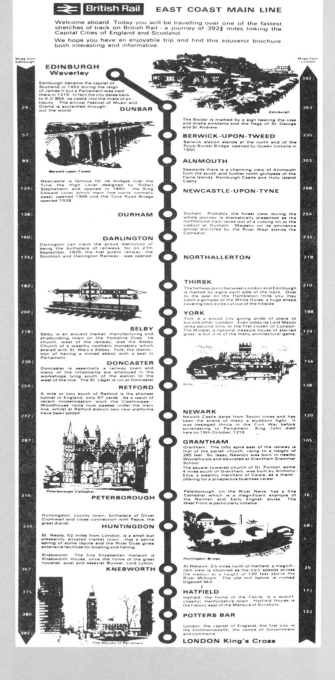

A montage of attractive Menu Cards used in L.N.E.R. Dining Cars. A typical Bill of Fare shows that you could get a good meal for 3/6d or less — but remember, the national average wage was under £2 per week!

# MENU

## Luncheon 3/6

Grape Fruit
or
Lentil Soup

---

Boiled Turbot    Shrimp Sauce
or
Pickled Fresh Herring

---

Minced Turkey & Poached Egg .
or
Roast Shoulder Mutton    Onion Sauce
Brussels Sprouts    Jacket & Mashed Potatoes

---

Gooseberry Pudding
Meringue Chantilly
Stewed Figs and Cream

English or
Scotch Meat
Only served
on this Car

---

Cheese etc.

---

Tea or Coffee 4d. Extra

Tuesday, January 5, 1937

## LUNCHEON 2/6

Fish or Joint with Vegetables
Sweets or Cheese

*A supplementary portion of any dish on the 3/6 Table d'Hote Menu will be served on request*

PASSENGERS ARE REQUESTED TO MAKE NO PAYMENT WITHOUT RECEIVING A BILL WHICH SHOULD BE WRITTEN OUT IN THEIR PRESENCE.

## RUNNING TIMES

### OF RESTAURANT CAR TRAINS LONDON TO SCOTLAND

**9th July to 30th September, 1934**

| Distance from King's Cross via York | via Leeds | | | WEEKDAYS | | | | | | | SUNDAYS | |
|---|---|---|---|---|---|---|---|---|---|---|---|---|
| | | | | | "The Flying Scotsman" | | | "The Queen of Scots" Pullman | | | | |
| | | | | A | B | B | C | D | E | F | G | H |
| Miles | Miles | | | a.m. | a.m. | a.m. | a.m. | a.m. | p.m. | p.m. | a.m. | p.m |
| — | — | King's Cross ... | ... dep. | ... | 10 0 | 10 0 | 10 5 | 11 20 | ... | 1 20 | 11 20 | 12 40 |
| 17¾ | 17¾ | Hatfield... ... | ... pass | ... | 10 25 | 10 25 | 10 31 | 11 44 | ... | 1 45 | 11 47 | 1 7 |
| 32 | 32 | Hitchin ... ... | ... arr. | ... | pass | pass | pass | pass | ... | pass | p.m. 12 4 | pass |
| | | ,, ... | ... dep. | ... | 10 39 | 10 39 | 10 45 | 11 57 | ... | 1 59 | 12 6 | 1 22 |
| 58¾ | 58¾ | Huntingdon (North) ... | pass | ... | 11 1 | 11 1 | 11 8 | p.m. 12 19 | ... | 2 22 | 12 35 | 1 47 |
| 76¼ | 76¼ | Peterborough (North) | arr. | ... | pass | pass | pass | pass | ... | pass | 12 55 | pass |
| | | ,, | ... dep. | ... | 11 19 | 11 19 | 11 26 | 12 37 | ... | 2 40 | 1 10 | 2 6 |
| 105½ | 105½ | Grantham ... | ... arr. | ... | pass | pass | p.m. 12 1 | pass | ... | 3 14 | 1 39 | pass |
| | | ,, ... | ... dep. | ... | 11 54 | 11 54 | 12 3 | 1 8 | ... | 3 16 | 1 44 | 2 43 |
| 120 | 120 | Newark ... | ... arr. | ... | p.m. ... | ... | ... | ... | ... | ... | 2 2 | ... |
| | | ,, ... | ... pass | ... | 12 10 | 12 9 | 12 18 | 1 20 | ... | 3 31 | ... | 3 10 |
| | | ,, ... | ... dep. | ... | ... | ... | ... | ... | ... | ... | 2 3 | ... |
| 138½ | 138 | Retford ... | ... arr. | ... | pass | pass | pass | pass | ... | pass | 2 25 | pass |
| | | ,, ... ... | ... dep. | ... | 12 31 | 12 29 | 12 38 | 1 38 | ... | 3 51 | 2 28 | 3 21 |
| 156 | 156 | Doncaster (Central) ... | arr. | ... | pass | pass | pass | pass | ... | pass | 2 49 | pass |
| | | ,, ,, | ... dep. | ... | 12 50 | 12 47 | 12 56 | 1 55 | ... | 4 9 | 2 54 | 3 40 |
| — | 175¾ | Wakefield (Westgate) | pass | ... | | | ... | 2 17 | ... | ... | .. | ... |
| — | 185¾ | Leeds (Central) | ... arr. | ... | | | ... | 2 34 | ... | ... | ... | ... |
| | | ,, ,, ... | ... dep. | 9L0 | Until 15th Sept. | Commences 17th Sept. | ... | 2 38 | 2L45 | ... | ... | ... |
| — | 195 | Arthington ... | ... pass | ... | | | ... | 2 55 | ... | ... | ... | ... |
| — | 204 | Harrogate ... | ... arr. | ... | | | ... | 3 7 | ... | ... | ... | ... |
| | | ,, ... ... | ... dep. | ... | | | ... | 3 10 | ... | ... | ... | ... |
| — | 215½ | Ripon ... ... | ... pass | ... | | | ... | 3 23 | ... | ... | ... | ... |
| 174¼ | — | Selby ... ... | ... arr. | ... | pass | pass | pass | ... | ... | pass | 3 17 | pass |
| | | ,, ... ... | ... dep. | ... | 1 11 | 1 7 | 1 16 | ... | ... | 4 30 | 3 20 | 4 1 |
| 188¼ | — | York ... ... | ... arr. | 9 32 | pass | pass | 1 36 | ... | 3 15 | 4 48 | 3 40 | 4 20 |
| | | ,, ... ... | ... dep. | 9 38 | 1 29 | 1 25 | 1 41 | ... | 3 25 | 4 52 | 3 50 | 4 27 |
| 210¼ | — | Thirsk ... ... | ... pass | 10 3 | 1 54 | 1 50 | 2 7 | ... | 3 52 | 5 17 | 4 16 | 4 54 |
| 218 | 229¼ | Northallerton ... | ... pass | 10 10 | 2 2 | 1 58 | 2 14½ | 3 39 | 4 0 | 5 25 | 4 24 | 5 2 |
| 232¼ | 243½ | Darlington ... | ... arr. | pass | pass | pass | pass | 3 55 | 4 15 | 5 40 | 4 40 | pass |
| | | ,, ... ... | ... dep. | 10 23 | 2 16 | 2 12 | 2 29 | 3 56 | 4 19 | 5 44 | 4 45 | 5 16 |
| 254¼ | 265½ | Durham ... | ... arr. | pass | pass | pass | pass | pass | 4 50 | pass | pass | pass |
| | | ,, ... | ... dep. | 10 48 | 2 42 | 2 38 | 2 55 | 4 24 | 4 53 | 6 12 | 5 15 | 5 44 |
| 268¼ | 279½ | Newcastle (Central) ... | arr. | 11 5 | pass | 2 56 | 3 13 | 4 42 | 5 12 | 6 31 | 5 35 | 6 3 |
| | | ,, ,, | ... dep. | 11 10 | 3 0 | 3 1 | 3 18 | 4 46 | 5 32 | 6 38 | 5 42 | 6 10 |
| 284¾ | 296 | Morpeth ... | ... arr. | pass | pass | pass | pass | pass | 5 58 | pass | pass | pass |
| | | ,, ... | ... dep. | 11 34 | 3 24 | 3 25 | 3 43 | 5 10 | 6 1 | 7 2 | 6 7 | 6 35 |
| 303¼ | 314½ | Alnmouth ... | ... arr. | ... | ... | ... | ... | ... | 6 25 | ... | ... | ... |
| | | ,, ... | ... pass | 11 55 | 3 45 | 3 45 | 4 3 | 5 30 | ... | ... | 6 29 | 6 55 |
| | | ,, .. | ... dep. | ... | ... | ... | ... | ... | 6 28 | 7 23 | ... | ... |
| 320 | 331¼ | Belford ... ... | ... pass | p.m. 12 13 | 4 3 | 4 3 | 4 21 | 5 48 | ... | 7 43 | 6 47 | 7 13 |
| | | ,, ... ... | ... dep. | ... | ... | ... | ... | ... | 6 55 | ... | ... | ... |
| 335¼ | 346½ | Berwick ... | ... arr. | pass | pass | pass | 4 38 | pass | 7 14 | 7 59 | 7 4 | pass |
| | | ,, ... ... | ... dep. | 12 29 | 4 20 | 4 20 | 4 40 | 6 4 | 7 16 | 8 1 | 7 6 | 7 30 |
| 363½ | 374¾ | Dunbar ... | ... arr. | ... | pass | pass | pass | pass | ... | pass | 7 42 | pass |
| | | ,, ... ... | ... dep. | ... | 4 54 | 4 54 | 5 15 | 6 36 | ... | 8 33 | 7 43 | 8 3 |
| 375 | 386¼ | Drem ... ... | ... pass | ... | ... | ... | ... | 6N50 | ... | 8N47 | ... | ... |
| 392¾ | 404 | Edinburgh (Waverley) | arr. | 1 35 | 5 30 | 5 30 | 5 50 | 7 15 | 8 30 | 9 10 | 8 20 | 8 40 |
| 440 | 451¼ | Glasgow (Queen Street) | arr. | 2 55 | ... | ... | 6 57 | 8 20 | 9 49 | 10 35 | ... | 9 50 |
| 440½ | 451¾ | Perth ... ... | ... arr. | 3 29 | ... | ... | 7 21 | ... | ... | 10 57 | ... | 10 27 |
| 452 | 463¼ | Dundee (Tay Bridge) | arr. | 3 29 | 7 33 | 7 33 | 7 33 | 8 56 | ... | ... | ... | 10 38 |
| 523¼ | 534½ | Aberdeen ... | ... arr. | 5 20 | 9 30 | 9 30 | 9 30 | ... | ... | ... | ... | ... |

*For particulars of Sleeping Car Trains see page 6*

**A**—Restaurant Car, Leeds to Glasgow. **B**—"The Flying Scotsman." Restaurant Cars, King's Cross to Edinburgh and Aberdeen. Through carriages to Aberdeen. **C**—Restaurant Car King's Cross to Edinburgh and Glasgow. Through carriage King's Cross to Perth, Glasgow and Aberdeen. **D**—"The Queen of Scots" Pullman, King's Cross to Glasgow. The usual Pullman supplements are charged by this train. **E**—Restaurant Car, Leeds to Glasgow. **F**—Restaurant Car, King's Cross to Edinburgh. **G**—Restaurant Car, King's Cross to Edinburgh. Conveys passengers for Edinburgh and beyond only. **H**—Restaurant Car, King's Cross to Edinburgh. Through carriage King's Cross to Glasgow. **N**—Calls at Drem when required to set down passengers. **L**—Leeds (New) Station.

was required to transform the performance of the "Pacifics". However, the first world record for the Gresley "Pacifics" was not in the realm of speed, for in 1928 they started running the whole way between London and Edinburgh without a stop at the head of the summer *"Flying Scotsman"* express. In order to make the jobs of driving and firing possible on such a long journey, a corridor tender was provided, which enabled the crews to change over while the train was speeding across the Plain of York, somewhere just south of Thirsk. At the time this non-stop run was introduced, the minimum times between London and Edinburgh, agreed after the 1888 Races, were still adhered to, so that the locomotives had to spin out the full 8¼ hours in each direction. From the crews' viewpoint, therefore, it was not high speed that was needed but good preparation to provide adequate lubrication, careful management of the water supplies, and accurate timing to ensure that out-of-course signal stops did not occur as a result of approaching important junctions too early. By the outbreak of World War II, however, the 1888 agreement had been mutually discarded and the "Non-stop" was taking only seven hours for the journey in each direction.

## World Beaters . . .

With the worst of the economic "depression" over, railway speeds on the East Coast Main Line started to rise during the 1930s, following the earlier lead of the Great Western with their *"Cheltenham Flyer"*, which by 1932 was averaging 71.3 m.p.h. from Swindon to Paddington. In 1934 and 1935 the L.N.E.R. carried out some test runs during which the locomotives *"Flying Scotsman"* and *"Papyrus"* recorded speeds of 100 and 108 m.p.h. descending Stoke Bank, near Peterborough. The former was the first fully authenticated "ton" achieved on the railways of this country, although a speed in that region was undoubtedly attained by the G.W.R. *"City of Truro"* as long ago as 1904.

Following the success of the L.N.E.R. trial runs, in the Autumn of 1935 the first of the

# LOCOMOTIVE RUNNING
# SUPERINTENDENTS' DEPARTMENT

**Memorandum to drivers and firemen concerned in non stop run, London to Edinburgh, and Edinburgh to London.**

Enginemen will change over at, or about Tollerton and when not working on the footplate will travel in a Third Class reserved compartment at the front of the train.

Each engine must carry an additional firing shovel.

In the event of there not being a supply of water in the troughs at both Wiske Moor and Lucker, it will be necessary for non-stop trains to stop at selected points in the North Eastern Area to obtain a supply of water. It has been decided that the trains will stop at the following points:-

| UP DIRECTION | DOWN DIRECTION |
|---|---|
| **Alnmouth –** Water column at South end of Up Platform. | **Thirsk –** Water column at North end of Down Platform. |
| **Darlington –** Water column on through roads just about South end of Up Platform and short of the signal bridge; this column supplies both the Up Main and the Up Independent. | **Alnmouth –** Water column at North end of Down Platform. |

Emergency engines will be at the following stations, and in case of failure enginemen must give the recognised engine whistles prior to reaching one of these points in order that the emergency engine will be in readiness:-

| DOWN JOURNEY | | UP JOURNEY | |
|---|---|---|---|
| King's Cross | Pacific Engine | Edinburgh | Pacific Engine |
| Hitchin | Atlantic Engine | Tweedmouth Shed | Atlantic Engine |
| Peterboro' | Atlantic Engine | Newcastle | Pacific Engine |
| Grantham | Pacific Engine | Darlington | Atlantic Engine |
| Doncaster | Pacific Engine | York | Atlantic Engine |
| York | Pacific Engine | Doncaster | Pacific Engine |
| Darlington | Atlantic Engine | Grantham | Pacific Engine |
| Newcastle | Pacific Engine | Peterboro' | Atlantic Engine |
| Tweedmouth Shed | Atlantic Engine | Hitchin | Atlantic Engine |

In the event of the emergency engine being utilised before the Enginemen's change-over point (Tollerton) is reached, both sets of men will travel on the footplate through to King's Cross or Edinburgh as the case may be.

The communicating doors in the tender must not be locked during the non-stop journey; on all other occasions the doors must be kept locked. The doors must be locked when the engines are stabled.

Drivers will be responsible for seeing that no unauthorised person is allowed on the engine; authorised persons will, in every case, be in possession of a special Engine Pass conspicuously marked "NON STOP", and issued by one or other of the undersigned:-

CHAS. M. STEDMAN, *North Eastern Area.*
S. GROOM, *Southern Area.*
G. A. MUSGROVE, *Scottish Area.*

**Locomotive Running Superintendents.**

**July 12th 1932.**

LNER

TAKE ME
BY
THE
FLYING
SCOTSMAN

LEAVES
KING'S CROSS
AT 10 A.M.
EVERY WEEK-DAY

WITH APOLOGIES
TO THE
SOUTHERN RAILWAY

FRANK H. MASON

"THE CO
ON THE EAST COA
IT'S QU
FULL INFORMATION FRO

**NATION"**
**TERING SCOTLAND**
**BY RAIL**
**ER OFFICE OR AGENCY**

# London · & · North · Eastern · Railway

## Passengers · of · the · Past

The Doctor said to Boswell "Sir,
It seemeth plain to me
That the Obvious Route to Scotland
Is from King's Cross L · N · E "

"Streamliners" was introduced. This was the *"Silver Jubilee"* express, which ran non-stop between Darlington and King's Cross, in each direction, averaging 70.4 m.p.h. over the 232.3 miles, making it the fastest long-distance train in the world. In contrast to today's "Inter-City 125" services (which are described in a later chapter), supplementary fares were charged for this prestige train, and were later officially stated to have paid for the whole cost of the rolling stock within two years. New articulated coaches were provided, and at the head of the silver-grey train was one of the first four Gresley streamlined "Pacifics". The characteristic wedge-shaped fronts of these locomotives became one of the most well-known and striking railway shapes, dominating the East Coast Route for the next 30 years.

Fast though the new schedule was, the Press demonstration run on 27 September 1935 behind *"Silver Link"* eclipsed all previous speeds achieved on rails in this country. It had been found that the braking power of the new train was such that speeds had to be restrained to 70 m.p.h. between Darlington and York, so the driver on the test run was encouraged to find out how much time he could save over the southern sections of the run. As a result, the speed remained at over 100 m.p.h. for 25 miles on end, and twice reached a new record of 112 m.p.h.

The commercial success of the *"Silver Jubilee"* illustrated that there was potential for other high-speed trains. Less than two years later the second of the East Coast streamlined expresses was introduced. This was the *"Coronation"*, which ran between London and Edinburgh in six hours, initially with one intermediate stop in each direction. The 71.9 m.p.h. booking over the 188.2 miles from King's Cross to York was the fastest yet to appear in a British timetable, beating the *"Cheltenham Flyer"* by a narrow margin. To rival the L.N.E.R's.*"Coronation"*, the L.M.S. introduced their streamliner, *"The Coronation*

*Scot"*, between Euston and Glasgow, and on their trial trip set up a new British railway speed record of 114 m.p.h., the train only narrowly escaping disaster when the braking on the approach to Crewe was left too late, and the subsequent rather hectic passage over the junctions outside the station resulted in some smashed crockery as well as involuntary embraces among those on the train.

The L.N.E.R. were anxious to regain the rail speed record. The opportunity came in July 1938 during brake tests with *"Mallard"*, one of the last batch of A4s to be turned out of Doncaster Works. Gresley, who had, by this time, been knighted for his services and had had the hundredth of his "Pacifics" named after him, wrote beforehand: "Whilst the brake trials will be made south of Peterborough, it is proposed to run the train to Barkston and back in order that a fast run down the bank from Stoke Tunnel may be recorded". While the train was being turned on the Barkston Triangle, the Westinghouse Brake Company's test team were told of the proposed attempt on the record, and offered the use of a taxi to take them to Peterborough if they wished. They all declined, and were to be among the small number of passengers who participated in setting up the World speed record for steam locomotives. At the summit of Stoke Bank the train was doing 74 m.p.h.; six miles later the speed was up to 116 m.p.h., and finally a peak of 126 m.p.h. was achieved—a feat never to be beaten in the steam era. So *"Mallard"* has a much honoured place in the National Railway Museum where it is probably the most popular single exhibit.

The last of the streamlined expresses, the *"West Riding Limited"*, was also introduced in 1937. Until the outbreak of World War II the trio operated with great regularity and were extremely popular with travellers. However, with the outbreak of hostilities in September 1939, the trains were withdrawn, and were never to reappear in their original guise.

Three A4s and an A3 roar north past Wood Green in the '30s with the "Flying Scotsman" and trains for Newcastle, Glasgow and Leeds.

Train signalling in 'steam days' involved the provision of massive gantries, arrayed with numerous semaphore signals, at main stations. Only in recent years has the work of replacing semaphores with modern multiple-aspect colour-light signals been completed on the East Coast Main Line.

A3 "Pacific" No. 60045 "Lemberg" heading north from Newcastle on a Leeds–Glasgow express in 1948, passing under the signal gantry which was replaced in the 1950s.

In 1905, the North Eastern Railway installed Hall's carbonic gas-operated signals between Alne and Thirsk. These automatically returned to the danger position after each train had passed, allowing trains to run faster and

on closer headways. Large stations, like York, required several signal boxes and no less than eight were required to control Main Line traffic. One of the smaller boxes was at Clifton, just north of the station; but Locomotive Yard

Box at the south end had what was reputedly the longest manually operated locking frame in the world, with 295 levers. Colour-light signals were installed between Alne and Thirsk in 1933.

## War and aftermath . . .

Under wartime conditions locomotive and track maintenance suffered, while the demands on the railways' capabilities to move passengers and freight reached new heights. Trains of more than 20 coaches were not infrequent on the East Coast Main Line, and on one occasion *"Silver Link"* was called upon to take no fewer than 25 bogies out of King's Cross. So long was this train that the engine and leading coaches were standing in Gasworks Tunnel!

After the War, the L.N.E.R. was determined to re-establish fast running as soon as possible. In May 1946 a round trip from King's Cross to Edinburgh was scheduled to test general condition of the track. On the return journey, *"Silver Fox"* achieved the first post-war "100" on the descent from Stoke Tunnel, but regular running of this standard was not to reappear for another decade or so.

Under the austerity conditions of immediate post-war years, transport systems came low on the National priority list, and with unemployment at a low level, the railways encountered serious difficulties in recruiting footplate and shed staff. These factors combined to produce a motive power crisis in 1951 on the Eastern Region as it then was, and drastic measures had to be taken to overcome it. Wholesale reallocations of locomotives took place, and arrangements were made to confine the operation of each top-link locomotive to two crews, the drivers having their own names on small plates which they were encouraged to put on the sides of the cabs. Some significant engineering improvements were made to the Gresley "Pacifics", which had by this stage been joined by the Thompson and Peppercorn locomotives of the same wheel arrangement, so that over the next few years speed standards over the East Coast Route improved once again.

The first post-war run timed at more than a mile-a-minute appeared in the timetable in 1949. The service was the *"North Briton"* on the stretch between Darlington and York. This was the

The result of extensive flooding in August

successor of the train which had, in 1922, seen the re-introduction of such bookings after World War I. By 1955, however, there were no fewer than 14 such bookings over the same section. The fastest run by steam appeared in the summer of 1958, the 44.1 miles being allowed 39 minutes at an average of 67.8 m.p.h., which represented the highest speed in the country at the time. This was achieved by a train that had been introduced only a year or two earlier, designed as one of a series to cater particularly for the businessman, and enabling him to make out and home journeys in a day—a pattern that was to continue in "Deltic" days (see the

ains of washed-out bridge near Reston.

succeeding chapter by Brian Perren).

## Through flood and storm . . .

Long-distance non-stop running had
recommenced on the East Coast Route in the
summer of 1948, when the *"Flying Scotsman"* once
again started plying between London and
Edinburgh without calling at intermediate stations.
In August that year, torrential rain in the Border
Counties, north of Berwick, caused numerous
bridges on the East Coast Line to be washed away
by the resulting floods. After the initial emergency
period, which saw the *"Flying Scotsman"* appearing

at Carlisle and following some very unusual
intermediate routes, trains were diverted from
Tweedmouth via Kelso and St. Boswells to
Edinburgh. Although booked to stop for a banking
engine and to take water, a few enterprising crews
on the *"Flying Scotsman"* ran through without
stopping over the longer and more difficult route,
setting up a new non-stop record of 408.6 miles. In
1949 the non-stop schedule was allocated to a new
train, running ahead of the *"Flying Scotsman"*, and
named the *"Capitals Limited"*. Because of the
repairs still in progress north of Berwick, the run
was eased to 8 hours, and it was an odd experience
to spend a third of a day on the same train, the
wheels of which never stopped turning. In 1953, to
mark the Coronation of Queen Elizabeth II, the
train was renamed the *"Elizabethan"*, and in the
following year the schedule was cut to 6 hours 30
minutes, which lifted the average speed just over
the 60 m.p.h. mark.

## Indian Summer . . .

During the late 1950s, steam locomotive
performance on the East Coast Route reached new
standards. These achievements took place across
the board, and were by no means confined to
prestige trains only. A fine indication of this
"performance in depth" is given by recounting the
exploits of the standard Class 9F heavy freight
locomotives, the last of which *"Evening Star"*, is
preserved in the National Railway Museum. The
class was outstandingly efficient on freight duties,
but was also called upon at times to work passenger
trains, as does *"Evening Star"* on specials today.
Summer Saturday train workings have always taxed
the motive power resources of the railways, and in
the 1950s it became common to roster a Class 9 to
haul a Saturdays-only train over the East Coast
Main Line. On one such occasion the locomotive
was recorded as achieving a speed of over 90 m.p.h.
descending Stoke Bank—a remarkable feat for
what is essentially a heavy freight design.

British Railways' Modernisation Plan,
announced in 1955, brought with it the intention to

replace steam by other forms of traction. Although electrification of the East Coast Route was included, the London Midland Region's Main Line out of Euston had priority. It was therefore diesel traction that was to take over from steam on the line from King's Cross to Edinburgh. The first diesel locomotives to become available were the most powerful that were being built under the "pilot" scheme—the 2,000 h.p. English Electric Type 4s, now known as the Class 40s. Diesel locomotives are far more efficient thermally than the reciprocating steam engine, and their full power output can be obtained with predictability, as and when required, no more effort being needed than moving the control lever round to the stop. However, a large steam locomotive in good "nick", with a fireman prepared to work hard, is capable of high power outputs, and an East Coast "Pacific" could, under these conditions, out-perform one of the Type 4s. The diesels in their early days were not too reliable either, one of the main difficulties being the train-heating boiler. As a result, steam locomotives, particularly the A4s, were often to be found working the diesel rosters, which called for a far greater weekly mileage than had ever before been achieved with steam, which rose once again to the demands of a new form of competition. In late 1958 *"Golden Fleece"* logged over 9,000 miles in 18 days, while a few months later *"Mallard"* clocked up 3,750 miles in a week, all on fast timings.

The East Coast authorities, however, had seen the potential of the English Electric "Deltic" locomotives of 3,300 h.p. and 22 had been ordered for use on principal expresses. Production difficulties resulted in their entry into service being delayed, and this gave steam the opportunity for a last final fling on the East Coast Route.

In the summer of 1961 I made a 10-day tour of railways in seven European countries to compare the different systems. The fastest speed recorded in the whole of the 3,000 miles was the 95 m.p.h. achieved behind the A4 *"Dominion of New Zealand"* hauling the *"Tees–Tyne Pullman"* over level track between Thirsk and York.

The steam locomotive has, throughout its existence, been the subject of great interest amongst the lay public in this country, and, during its final years on British Railways, many special trains were organised by railway societies. Two of these must serve as a final reminder of the glories of steam power over the East Coast Route. The Stephenson Locomotive Society, founded in 1909 as the first nation-wide society devoted to locomotive matters, celebrated their Golden Jubilee in 1959 by organising a special train from King's Cross to Doncaster and back. One of the society's members, the King's Cross Top Link driver Bill Hoole, was in charge of his regular A4 *"Sir Nigel Gresley"*, and the Eastern Region authorities relaxed the official 90 m.p.h. speed limit over a number of sections of the line. On the down trip the train accelerated over the last stages of the climb to Stoke to achieve a final speed of 82 m.p.h., which represented a far higher power output than could have been achieved by one of the Type 4 diesels. On the return journey the descent of the famous bank was the focus of great excitement, and everyone on the train concentrated on the mileposts as the speed steadily increased, until finally the train achieved a post-war record of 112 m.p.h. The day's exhilaration was not over, however, as later in the journey, just as all aboard were relaxing, another 100 m.p.h. sprint was achieved, this time over completely level track without any aid from gravity as there had been on the descent from Stoke.

Just over five years later came the last Main Line steam run from King's Cross. The Stephenson Locomotive Society combined forces with the Railway Correspondence and Travel Society to promote the *"Jubilee Requiem"*. The A4 *"Union of South Africa"* worked a round trip to Newcastle, and through no fault of the engine, the outward journey was badly delayed. Every seat on the train had been applied for twice over, and the operating authorities kept the tracks clear on the homeward journey to give the locomotive a last chance to show what steam could achieve over the East Coast

Main Line. Stops were made at York and Peterborough, and each of the three sections was run at an average of over 60 m.p.h. start-to-stop. In the darkness of the late October evening, the locomotive was given its head down Stoke Bank, reaching the very creditable maximum of 96 m.p.h. Eventually the train stopped in King's Cross no less than 26 minutes early.

For the crowds that night who thronged the end of the platforms at King's Cross as the A4 backed out and clattered over the points into Gasworks Tunnel, the final long blast on her distinctive chime whistle must have been a poignant reminder of the great contribution made by steam power to speed on the East Coast Main Line.

Water-troughs, enabling locomotives to replenish their tenders at speed, first appeared in the 19th Century to extend the range of small contemporary locomotives. From the 1920s they made it possible for the "Pacifics" to run non-stop between King's Cross and Newcastle or Edinburgh.

# THE DELTIC ERA

By Brian Perren, Contributor, "Modern Railways"

What does the Deltic Era conjure up in the minds of those who have savoured it or been closely associated with it?

It was an era when British Rail parted company with the legacies of the past and entered, in the early Sixties, into a period when passengers were enticed on to trains, not by the magic lure of steam, but because a modern fast railway could, for business or pleasure, satisfy their travel needs.

The Deltic Era—the 15 years from 1962 to 1977—will be remembered for vast physical changes on the East Coast Main Line brought about by a new confidence and Management style. It will be recalled, too, as the time when the legacy of introspection and self doubt generated by the Marples–Beeching regime was discarded and British Rail became an outgoing, aggressive organisation successfully marketing an excellent national product called Inter-City. Above all, it was during this period that British Rail's marketing men were clearly seen to become customer rather than product orientated, when rail managers began to capitalise on growth opportunities, to concentrate upon improving the generic product that would satisfy customer needs.

With the replacement of steam by diesel, the building of new passenger coaches and investment in track and signalling, the outstanding L.N.E.R. achievements of the Thirties were gradually eclipsed by the new norms of the Sixties. New perameters were established. In the Seventies the average time of all daytime trains between King's Cross and Edinburgh was less than six hours—the schedule of the steam-hauled *"Coronation"* streamline train, running only once daily on Mondays-to-Fridays and only accessible on payment of a supplement. While three-figure speeds were occasionally achieved by steam-hauled trains in exceptional circumstances, by 1973 eighty-five per cent of the East Coast Route between King's Cross and Newcastle had been upgraded and resignalled so that 100 m.p.h. was the line speed norm on a day-to-day regularly scheduled basis. The introduction of air-conditioned coaches was not only a significant advance on any previous passenger stock but B.R. became the first railway in Western Europe to offer this standard of comfort to all passengers, first and second class, on a universal basis without payment of a supplement. In 1938 the L.N.E.R. established

on one glorious occasion a world record for steam of 126 m.p.h.; 40 years on, in 1978, 125 m.p.h. will become the normal maximum speed for most daytime trains on the East Coast Main Line.

## A new image

What we have called the Deltic Era on the East Coast Main Line is of course a part of the national Inter-City era. Railway Managements have always had a good sense of publicity but the entire approach to selling travel by rail during the past 15 years has changed as dramatically as the

equipment and infrastructure. Before the second World War railway publicity tended to be based on two main themes: the romance of a journey by a crack steam-hauled express and the part played by the railway in the annual family holiday to the sea—probably, in most cases, the only occasion in the year when the average family made a long journey by train. But in the Sixties B.R. had to adjust to the new conditions of the mass popular travel market. Widespread private car ownership and package tours by jet aircraft to exotic destinations abroad were incompatible with the

nglish Electric who thought of putting an engine off a motor gunboat into a locomotive . . . . "

*G. F. Fiennes in 1967.*

past romance of the steam age.

Sensibly, B.R. adopted a new image, partly facilitated by the Beeching policy of recruiting senior executives, particularly marketing men, into British Rail from the private sector. A first class marketing organisation, both at Board and Regional level, was able to develop and sell a product tailored to meet the customers' needs. The most important event in this period was the choice of Inter-City as a national brand name, which could be used in building a house style, corporate identity programme, advertising and promotion. Inter-City

was promoted nationally in T.V. commercials, and in press and poster campaigns. An attractive young model, Monica, who was successfully featured in several Inter-City campaigns, became so well-known in her own right that she had to cope with a large mail from other young ladies wanting to know where she bought her clothes!

Sound promotion attracted additional traffic and Inter-City made a successful entry into the package tour business with its own Golden Rail inclusive holidays by train. During the Seventies B.R's. marketing organisation referred to

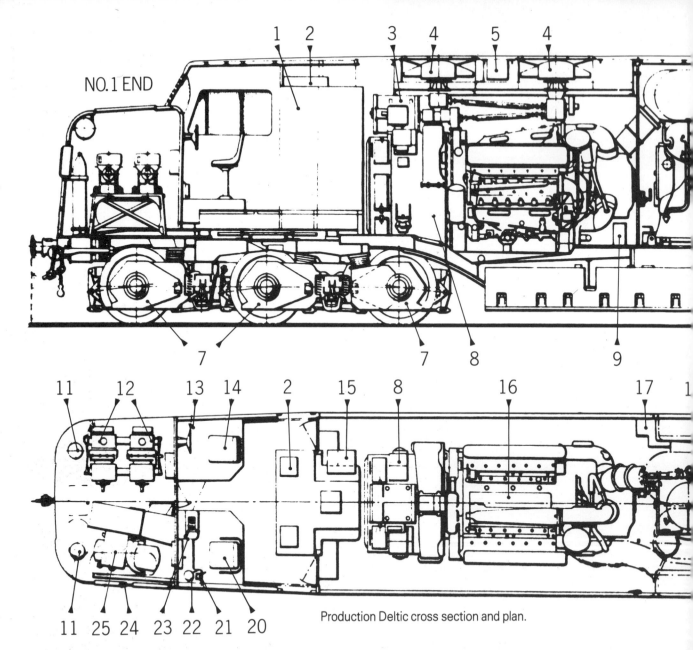

NO.1 END

Production Deltic cross section and plan.

1—Control equipment cubicle
2—Resistors
3—Auxiliary generators
4—Cooling fan
5—Header tank, water system
6—Route indicator
7—Traction motor
8—Main generator
9—Lubricating oil tank
10—Water pick-up
11—Fire-extinguisher, $CO_2$
12—Brake exhauster
13—Handbrake
14—Seat for assistant driver
15—Cooker
16—Deltic engine

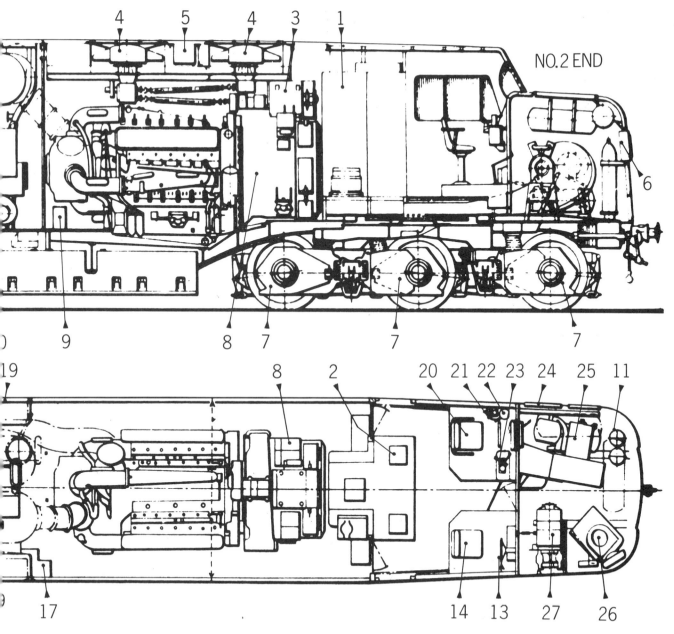

NO.2 END

4   5   4   3   1                                    6

9                    8   7          7              7

19        8   2      20 21 22 23 24 25 11

17              14 13 27 26

17—Water tank filling duct      21—Air-brake valve        25—Traction-motor blower
18—Train-heating boiler         22—Vacuum-brake valve     26—Toilet
19—Engine air filters           23—Controller             27—Air compressor
20—Driver's seat                24—Traction-motor air filters

"customers" rather than passengers, "product" and not train service, "product quality" instead of punctuality and cleanliness and "prices" instead of fares. As Travel Centres replaced booking offices and travel lounges replaced waiting rooms, B.R. began to evaluate their business in terms of market share, and brand names such as Motorail, Golden Rail and Sleepers. A new era had arrived. British Rail was now an outgoing marketing organisation viewing the entire business process as a tightly integrated effort aimed at discovering, arousing, creating and satisfying customer needs.

## Deltic arrival

Most of the major modernisation projects initiated by B.R. in the second-half of the Fifties originated in the British Transport Commission's 1955 Modernisation Plan—a published set of proposals involving an expenditure of £1,200m. —but the decision to purchase 22 Deltic locomotives was a spin-off from the basic plan and was not specified as part of the original prospectus.

The East Coast Main Line between King's Cross and York, or possibly Newcastle, was, together with the main line from Euston to Crewe, Manchester and Liverpool, listed as a candidate for electrification. In the event, the L.M.R. route received priority. Moreover, since electrification work was now in hand on the Kent Coast; between Liverpool Street and Enfield, Chingford and Bishops Stortford; Colchester and Clacton; and Fenchurch Street to Tilbury and Southend, it became apparent that neither B.R's. design staff nor the capacity of the electrical engineering supply industry could cope with electrification of the East Coast Route until the Sixties. This left the route in a planning vacuum and long distance passenger business was declining. The boom in post war motor-car ownership was well under way, a national motorway network was in prospect, turboprop aircraft were in use between London, Newcastle and Edinburgh.

Despite improvements in speed and frequency introduced in 1958—which gave the East Coast "Pacifics" an Indian Summer—the journey time on offer would soon be uncompetitive. Even these times would have to be slowed to cope with pre-electrification engineering work. Retention of the East Coast passenger business could no longer await electrification, the timing and possibility of which was becoming increasingly uncertain—and an alternative strategy was a matter of urgency. East Coast Management had given much thought to the standards of service required to be competitive —the 60 m.p.h. journey had to be lifted to at least 75 m.p.h. This was perfectly feasible, of course, with electrification, but not with any of the diesel-electric locomotives so far ordered by the B.T.C., none of which exceeded 2,000 h.p.

Meanwhile, anticipating the demise of steam, English Electric had built as a private venture costing £250,000, a new high-powered but relatively light-weight diesel locomotive prototype known as the "Deltic". Space does not permit a full description of the Deltic locomotive (it has been fully documented elsewhere) but its basic features

Side elevation of a production Deltic.

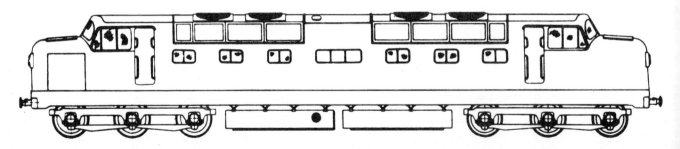

Prototype Deltic under test in 1958.

were just what the East Coast Management were seeking—its weight of 130 tons could be reduced to under 100 tons to produce wider route availability, and it had a maximum speed of 105 m.p.h. A major disadvantage—so far as B.R's. engineers were concerned—was the high cost of maintenance.

Purchase of a fleet of Deltic locomotives, costing £200,000 each, was, therefore, an extremely controversial proposal. It was with due prudence that the East Coast Management prepared their financial case. Since they did not wish to weaken their case for long-term electrification—still a possibility as late as 1959—the financial case was based on a reduction of operating costs with no credit assumed for additional business. While B.R. knew from experience that a typical suburban electrification was likely tò double revenue, it was only in later years—following the outstanding success of the L.M.R. West Coast electrification —that new techniques could be used to assess the market impact of Inter-City train service improvements.

Had the East Coast Route Management been able to forecast the subsequent growth of business in the Sixties the case for a larger fleet of Deltics for an expanded East Coast service would undoubtedly have been made.

By the Seventies the Deltic fleet was sufficient only to cover less than half the daytime Inter-City departures to and from King's Cross. But the case for the Deltic, based purely on operating economies, was staggering. Eastern Region had had several years experience of redrafting time-tables, giving a shift of emphasis towards locomotive and rolling stock utilisation rather than supposed public demand, with particular success in East Anglia. Many of the basic principles of Inter-City operating philosophy had their origins in the 1951 "Britannia Pacific" timetable between Liverpool Street and Norwich.

Studies showed that 22 Deltics, each running 200,000 miles a year, could replace 55 less powerful steam locomotives, saving a large number of locomotive and shed staff and providing heavier train formations which would reduce the need for reliefs. Faster running on the Main Line would produce better utilisation of coaches and reduce the number of train sets. English Electric had meanwhile cut the weight of the locomotive to suit a wide route availability and proposed a novel maintenance contract based on mileages achieved in service.

Thus, in 1958, an order for 22 Deltics was placed with English Electric with delivery expected in 1960 and 1961. In the event the first production Deltic did not arrive until May 1961. The balance of the fleet was delivered over the rest of the year to complete an allocation of eight locomotives to Finsbury Park depot London, six to Gateshead and eight to Haymarket in Edinburgh. The allocation was basically for maintenance purposes but the 22 locomotives were operated on common-user basis throughout the East Coast Main Line.

The original target date for a full accelerated Deltic service was 1961, but the phase-in programme was made in three stages. To meet a long-standing promise to a deputation from Dundee, who had complained about late delivery of mail in the city owing to poor punctuality of the overnight 19.30 from King's Cross to Aberdeen, this train was given Deltic haulage from the summer of 1961 when it was accelerated by 55 mins. to Edinburgh and beyond. The locomotive for this train worked to a special single roster comprising the 10.00 from Edinburgh to King's Cross (*"The Flying Scotsman"*), but still scheduled in steam timings, and returning north with the 19.30.

A second batch of important business trains was speeded up in September and the full service was introduced on 18 June 1962.

The Up "Tees–Tyne Pullman" leaving one of the first 100 m.p.h. stretches of the East Coast Main Line between Stoke and Lolham in 1964.

Welcome aboard
*on the*
First run of the Fastest-ever
scheduled service
*from*
London
*to*
Darlington and Newcastle

Monday 4 May 1970

## Turning point

Introduction of the Deltic timetable in June 1962, probably marked the turning point in the declining reputation of B.R. in post-war years. By 1960 the Government, in the person of the Minister of Transport, Ernest Marples, did not see a rosy future for rail transport and, based on false assumptions derived by comparison with the situation in the United States where long-distance passenger trains had been displaced by airlines and the long-distance bus, had stopped many capital investment projects outstanding at the time. Even completion of L.M.R. electrification southwards from Crewe to London was at risk but agreement to complete the project was eventually given; but Great Northern suburban electrification was halted and did not see completion for another 15 years. June 1962 was important because the new East

A series of promotions have highlighted each major improvement in East Coast Main Line services. A glass of champagne and a souvenir folder made this a trip to remember in 1970.

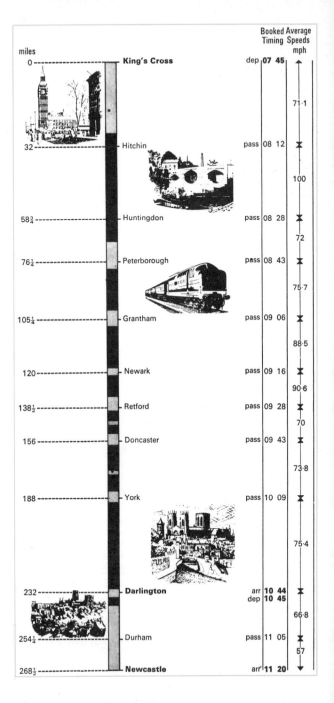

| miles | | Booked Timing | Average Speeds mph |
|---|---|---|---|
| 0 | King's Cross | dep 07 45 | |
| | | | 71·1 |
| 32 | Hitchin | pass 08 12 | |
| | | | 100 |
| 58¾ | Huntingdon | pass 08 28 | |
| | | | 72 |
| 76¼ | Peterborough | pass 08 43 | |
| | | | 75·7 |
| 105¼ | Grantham | pass 09 06 | |
| | | | 88·5 |
| 120 | Newark | pass 09 16 | |
| | | | 90·6 |
| 138½ | Retford | pass 09 28 | |
| | | | 70 |
| 156 | Doncaster | pass 09 43 | |
| | | | 73·8 |
| 188 | York | pass 10 09 | |
| | | | 75·4 |
| 232 | Darlington | arr 10 44 dep 10 45 | |
| | | | 66·8 |
| 254¼ | Durham | pass 11 05 | |
| | | | 57 |
| 268½ | Newcastle | arr 11 20 | |

# A champagne occasion . . .

Today's a champagne occasion for the Eastern Region of British Rail, and for our passengers too. It is, in fact, a day for the record books.

You are travelling on the first run of the fastest-ever rail service from King's Cross to Darlington and Newcastle. Starting with this train, the journey times of regular scheduled Inter-City services on this route have been cut by up to 15 minutes. Northbound, this train will now take only 3 hours 35 minutes for the journey to Newcastle; only 2 hours 59 minutes to Darlington.

We thought you should have a memento of the occasion. This card gives some information about the journey times and indicates the sections of line where 100mph running is now possible.

Over three-quarters of a million pounds have been spent on engineering during the past year to smooth out curves and give new track alignments near Huntingdon, at Grantham, near Doncaster, near Darlington and north and south of Durham. In all, some 200 miles of the 268 between London and Newcastle have been brought to 100mph running standards.

And the work goes on – better signalling systems to improve punctuality, more modern coaches for your comfort.

## British Rail is travelling

Coast timetable established a hitherto unknown standard of speed over long distances and showed that the advantages of modernisation, so often promised, were now a reality. Deltic power was allocated to all daytime Anglo-Scottish trains, important West Riding and Newcastle business trains and overnight sleeper services; other trains were hauled by lower-powered diesel locomotives and some were steam-hauled. Highlights of the service were the introduction of three six-hour trains each way between King's Cross and Edinburgh *("Elizabethan", "Flying Scotsman"* and *"Talisman")*; the accelerated 15-coach 530 ton *"Aberdonian"* and the highest ever average point-to-point speed to be booked in Great Britain— a 35 min. run at 75.6 m.p.h. by the southbound *"Tees–Tyne Pullman"* between Darlington and York. The new timetable got off to a flying start with well-justified publicity—an appropriate send-off for the Centenary run of the *"Flying Scotsman"* on the new six-hour schedule. A significant step forward in the quest for speed on the East Coast Route had been taken.

## Doing the "Ton"

The first four years of the full Deltic timetable were the initial stage of what was to become a 10-year period of progressive improvements to East Coast Inter-City services during which developments were planned, implemented, and consolidated before the next set of changes was introduced. By April 1966 some sections of route had been upgraded for 100 m.p.h. speeds and further cuts in journey times were made. The *"Flying Scotsman"* was speeded up by 10 minutes to complete the journey in 5 hr. 50 min. northbound (southbound 5 hr. 49 min.) and most other trains had several minutes cut from their journeys. The 35-minute Darlington–York timing for the *"Tees–Tyne Pullman"* mentioned above was pared by two minutes to 33 minutes, thereby giving the East Coast Route its first 80 m.p.h. start-to-stop timing. Compared with 1962, when a number of trains had to depend on 2,000 h.p. diesels or steam

haulage, the average speed of all East Coast trains was much higher. But the highlight of the 1966 timetable was the introduction of the "Deltic-plus-eight" concept. A market research study in the West Riding area had indicated that there was good business potential from regular air travellers and car users who would be prepared to change to rail if certain features of the service were made more attractive. The conclusion was that— apart from speed itself—passengers required a high standard of service on the train; meals at every seat; quiet riding and reliable heating in the winter months. To test market the results of the survey, it was decided to divide the morning business service from the West Riding into separate services from Leeds and Bradford to King's Cross with return trains in the afternoon.

Substantial acceleration of trains between Leeds and King's Cross was, however, difficult. Compared with pre-war, when the impact of coal mining subsidence was less severe, really fast running between Leeds and Doncaster was no longer possible—any reduction in journey time had to be made between Doncaster and King's Cross. This could be achieved only by reducing the train formation to 280 tons (eight vehicles) which, with Deltic haulage, gave a worthwhile acceleration. To meet other requirements in the market survey, the formation of each train comprised a brake first, two open firsts with meal service at each seat, a kitchen/restaurant car, a buffet car and three open seconds. The morning trains left Leeds at 07.25, reaching King's Cross at 10.05, and 07.36 from Bradford, due in King's Cross at 10.40; return departures were 15.20 for Bradford and 15.55 for Leeds. All four trains loaded well and developed new business.

Encouraged by this success, more Deltic-plus-eight trains were introduced in 1967. A service was provided from Newcastle at 07.25, returning from King's Cross at 18.00. Southbound, with a single stop at Darlington, the timing was 3 hr. 50 min. (69.9 m.p.h.); northbound the timing was 3 hr. 55 min., with an additional call at

Durham. The West Riding service was expanded to three Deltic-plus-eight trains each way between King's Cross and Leeds in addition to the Bradford service which was unchanged but retimed. To further develop the appeal of these trains the first deliveries to the East Coast Route of British Rail's Mark IIa air-braked passenger coaches were allocated to them.

When planes are grounded and motorways treacherous, the trains still get through. "Argyll and Sutherland Highlander" on the 11.30 King's Cross to Leeds in February 1971.

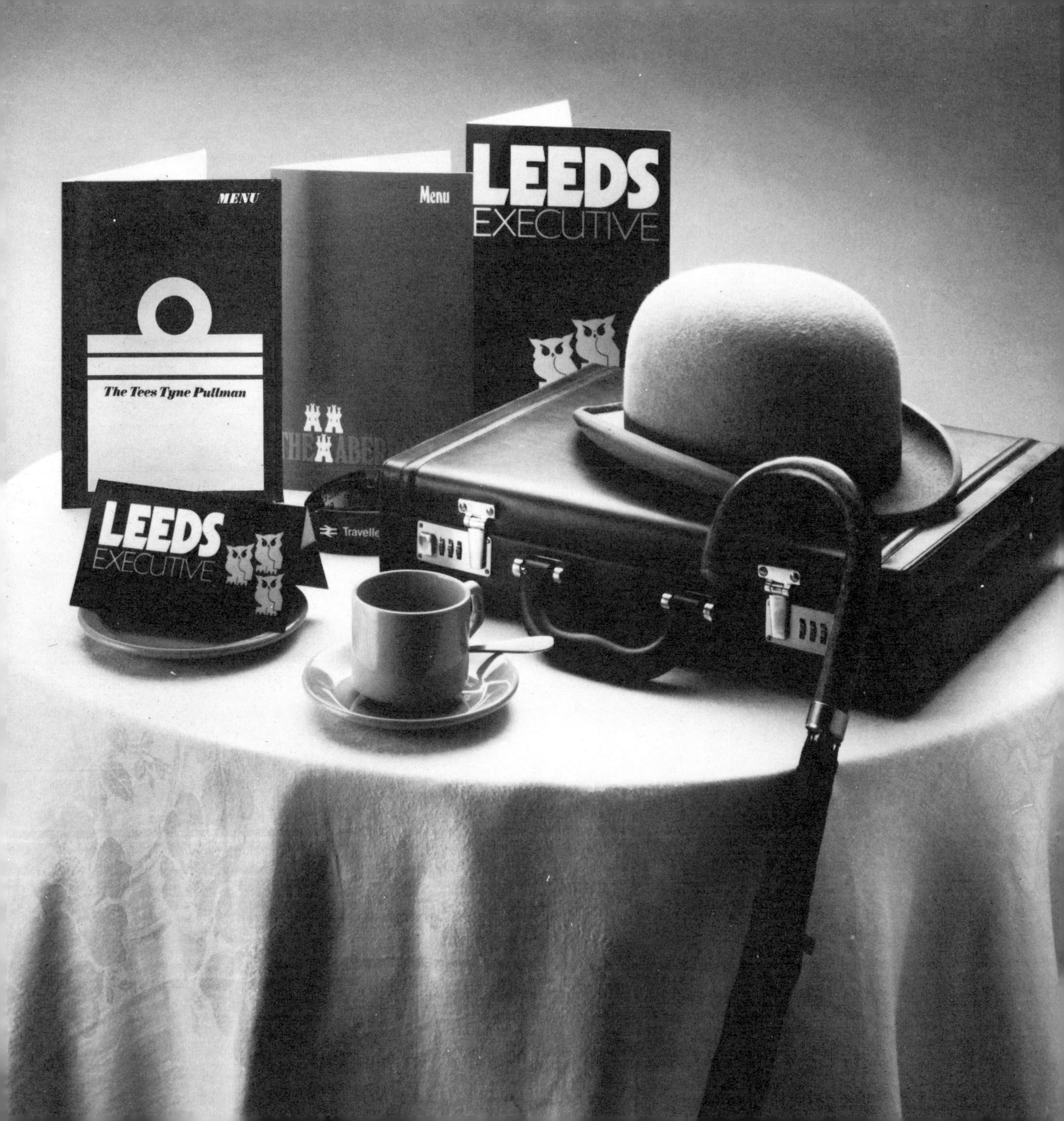
MENU
The Tees Tyne Pullman
Menu
LEEDS
EXECUTIVE
LEEDS
EXECUTIVE
Travelle

# Passenger comfort

The East Coast Main Line has long been renowned for the elegance and comfort of the passenger coaches on its front rank long-distance services. Special sets of coaches were built in pre-war L.N.E.R. days for the three streamline trains and the *"Flying Scotsman"*; some of these cars were still in service at the start of the diesel era. Pullman cars also ran in the Thirties on the *"Queen of Scots"* and *"Yorkshire Pullman"* services. Pullman services were, in fact, extended in the Fifties and Sixties, using new cars built for the East Coast Main Line. Following Nationalisation it was, of course, inevitable that rolling stock design should be standardised throughout B.R. Development occurred in two phases—a first series of Mark I standard vehicles, and subsequent improvement of these designs to form the Mark II fleet. By the end of 1964, 71 Mark II coaches were in service. The dramatic progress in passenger comfort which was to be a feature of the Mark II fleet had its origins in the XP64 train built by B.R. in 1964. This project comprised eight new passenger coaches—three corridor firsts, two corridor seconds and three open seconds—and four refurbished standard Mark I coaches. A 12-coach train was formed, making its debut in June 1964 on the *"Talisman"* service to test design and assess public reaction. The XP64 train had many innovations—improved bogies, thermal and acoustic insulation, pressure heating and ventilation, improved toilets, wide double-glazed windows, wider doors, bigger vestibules and improved lighting. Also of special interest were wide, jack-knife, double-folding doors and a new toilet basin with a controlled spray tap.

Further design work was undertaken in 1964 and 1965 before production of the next batch of 133 Mark II open seconds for L.M.R. electrification in 1966, these coaches including a number of the XP64 features. By the end of 1966 a total of 322 Mark II coaches had been built and design work and construction was organised on a continuing basis. The next batch of 400 coaches was a development of the basic Mark II vehicle aimed at boosting comfort and reducing vehicle weight. This Mark IIa design included many new features. Included as standard items were ergonomically-designed seating, individual seat lights, greater sound and heat insulation, pressure ventilation, and a foot operated toilet flush and hand basin spray.

By 1967 developments in insulation enabled remarkable improvements to be made in noise reduction within the vehicle; multi-thickness floors provided an effective barrier to noises from bogie, track and the operation of brakes. A new design of vestibule end and gangway, incorporating foldaway end doors, gave a compact and much neater appearance as well as reducing noise and preventing draught. Weight reduction, essential not only to minimise running expenses but also to reduce building costs, was achieved by the highly-successful B4 bogie, the employment of light alloys, and plastics instead of traditional materials, and the use of glass fibre seat-shells and foam seat fillings instead of steel and timber seat frames and sprung interiors. Despite the inclusion of double-glazing and pressure ventilation, the average weight of the Mark II coaches was as low as 31½ tons compared with 35 tons average for the final versions of Mark I stock.

"Executive Travel"—Improved services, speed and comfort convinced the businessman of the advantages of rail travel. Named trains, for many years a feature of the East Coast Main Line, were given a boost in the early '70s by a new range of attractive publicity material.

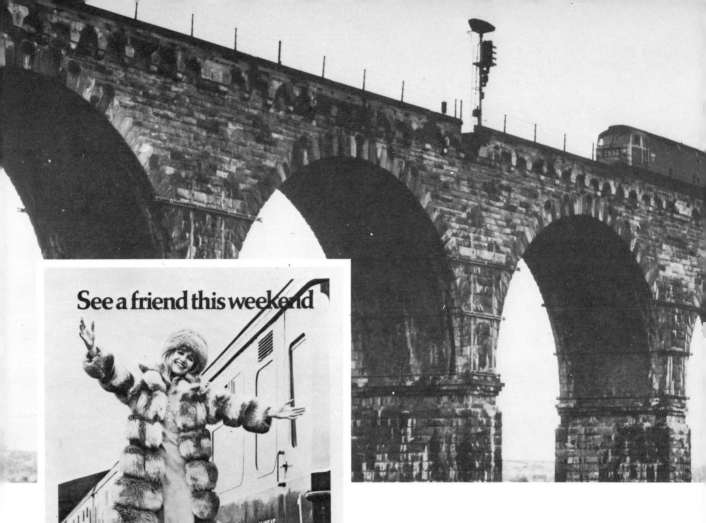

**See a friend this weekend**

There are many rail travel bargains-ask for them.

# Inter-City-a

This catchy slogan was one of many used to help advertise a wide range of reduced fares, and to motivate people to travel by train, for leisure or pleasure – to see friends or relations, or for shopping trips. Press advertisements, television commercials, folders and posters carried the message into most homes. The poster depicting the model, Monica, was very popular.

# y from it all and home again

Edinburgh was one of the most popular places which could be visited with a
Travel Bargain ticket. A Class 47 heads an Anglo–Scottish train over the
Royal Border Bridge at Berwick.

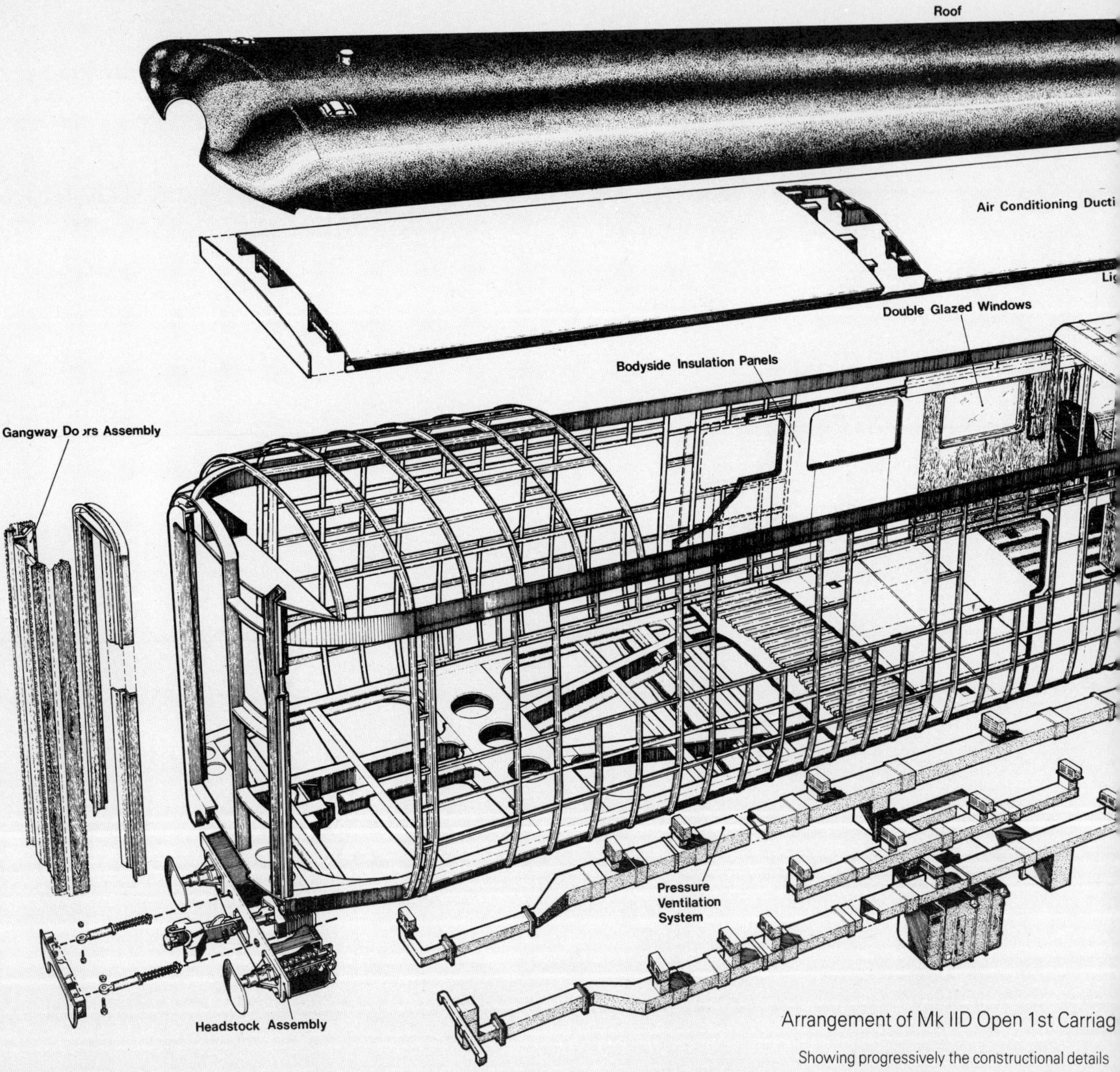

Roof

Air Conditioning Ducti

Li

Double Glazed Windows

Bodyside Insulation Panels

Gangway Doors Assembly

Pressure
Ventilation
System

Headstock Assembly

Arrangement of Mk IID Open 1st Carriag

Showing progressively the constructional details

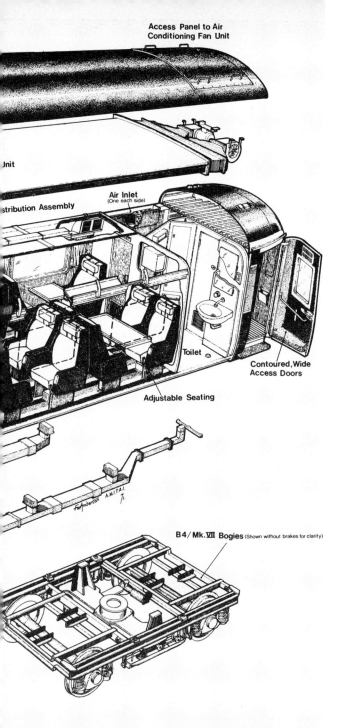

**Access Panel to Air Conditioning Fan Unit**

Unit

**Air Inlet** (One each side)

stribution Assembly

**Toilet**

**Contoured, Wide Access Doors**

**Adjustable Seating**

AMITAI 71

**B4/Mk.VII Bogies** (Shown without brakes for clarity)

In the realms of train working, the most important development in the Mark IIa design was a changeover to air braking. Although air braking was already used extensively in some areas, like the Southern Electric and G.E. steam suburban services, its use on long-distance locomotive-hauled trains was precluded by high costs of converting locomotives and the sheer size of the passenger fleet.

By the mid-Sixties, however, Inter-City services were covered by a smaller fleet of intensively-used sets of stock working in fixed formations, and the elimination of steam had simplified the conversion of motive power. Against this background, B.R. decided to adopt air braking for all new rolling stock. Even with a reduced coaching fleet, the changeover to air brakes had to be carefully planned. The first formation of Mark IIa stock and Mark I air-braked ancillary vehicles started service on the East Coast Main Line in November 1967, covering the 07.25 Newcastle to King's Cross and 18.00 northbound return service. During 1968 a number of the East Coast Main Line trains were wholly changed over to Mark IIa stock with very favourable public response.

The next major phase in the Mark II programme included two significant developments —introduction of an open first design and of full air-conditioning for all future Inter-City coaches. Air-conditioned coaches were designated Mark IId and subsequent vehicles, with detailed modifications, Mark IIe or f.

The first Mark IId coaches were introduced in 1972 on the East Coast Main Line and immediately set new standards of passenger amenity. As their designers rightly predicted, the elimination of all outside sound was the post-war breakthrough in passenger comfort. A total of 1,947 Mark II vehicles were built, of which 975 were Mark IId, e or f, equipped with air-conditioning. By the end of 1972, 24 of the 34 sets of stock required for East Coast Route daytime trains were formed with Mark IId vehicles; the balance was made up with Mark IIa and Mark I vacuum braked sets. An allocation of 40 additional Mark IIf coaches was made to the East Coast Route during 1973, making it possible to programme Mark IIa sets for the York–Aberdeen train and the South Humberside services. As new building continued, B.R. reallocated stock as part of a national "cascade" plan so that the premier routes had the latest stock, older stock was transferred to less important routes and old Mark I stock was withdrawn. By 1975 all East Coast sets were air-conditioned.

## On the tracks

The situation had been reached, however, where the advances in journey times made in the 1967/1968 timetable were the best that the East Coast Route could offer without investment in line speed improvements. The Deltics were the first diesel locomotives capable of 100 m.p.h. running but in 1967 this speed was only possible over 77 miles of route between King's Cross and Newcastle. With traffic between the North-east and London vulnerable to air and motorway competition, the amenity improvements of Mark IIa stock had to be matched by further cuts in journey times if B.R. were to retain the business. Between 1963 and 1967 B.R's. share of the London–Newcastle market had advanced from 44 to 48 per cent but was now starting to level off. Motorway competition had also kept rail's share of the Leeds–London market in the same period to 46 per cent.

The immediate objective was to eliminate some of the permanent speed restrictions which were precluding optimum performance of existing traction and rolling stock. Studies showed that up to 15 minutes could be saved between King's Cross and Newcastle if about £750,000 was spent on line speed improvements, and even more time could be saved if the long-standing restriction of 20 m.p.h. through Peterborough could be removed. Project plans were produced and submitted for approval in two stages. Stage One—approved in 1969—covered the following work—realignment at Offord—

East Coast Inter-City travel of the '70s. Deltic No. 55016 "Gordon Highlander" and the Mark IID air-conditioned coaches on the northbound "Flying Scotsman" at Newcastle.

where the course of the River Ouse was altered to conform with the railway's realignment— gave an increase in speed from 70 to 100 m.p.h.; realignment of the north end of Grantham station raised the speed there from 70 to 95 m.p.h.; improvements at Bawtry permitted 80 m.p.h.; realignment and rationalisation at Durham raised the speed from 30 to 50 m.p.h. and major works to realign the main line through a new location at Newton Hall gave an improvement of 55 to 85 m.p.h. Also involved in this stage were minor

(Skelton)–Darlington (Croft) (39). A maximum speed of 95/100 m.p.h. over 60 per cent of the route between King's Cross and Newcastle made a considerable contribution to time saving but the effect of improvements at locations like Durham, where speeds were more modest, also saved valuable minutes, particularly for Class 47 locomotives with their slower rate of acceleration.

Expenditure for Stage Two of the line speed improvements was £2½m. The major item was the long-awaited remodelling and resignalling of Peterborough North station. This was a mammoth task with the main operating benefit being elimination of the 20 m.p.h. "dog-leg" curve and the provision of new through 100 m.p.h. tracks for non-stopping trains. A series of civil engineering works was also implemented in the King's Cross area between Wood Green and Woolmer Green. The up fast and slow lines were lowered and realigned in the original Potters Bar tunnel and track was strengthened and realigned at several places south of Woolmer Green. At Hatfield tracks were slewed and realigned as part of the station rebuilding so that line speed could be raised from 80 to 100 m.p.h. When all this was completed another 19 miles of route from Wood Green to Woolmer Green were upgraded to 100 m.p.h. to link up with the section from there to Holme, giving a continuous high-speed section of 66 miles. Realignment of track at Saltersford and between High Dyke and Grantham enabled this location to be upgraded to 100 m.p.h.

Further north, a major improvement was made at Selby. Here the long-standing speed restriction through Selby station and round the curve to Barlby Junction was subject to a restriction of 45/50 m.p.h. As the line speed either side of Selby was 100 m.p.h. its restriction had a severe impact on the speed of Inter-City trains. Because of the time taken to accelerate from 45 m.p.h., northbound trains could only achieve 100 m.p.h. for a brief period over the 10-mile section on to Chaloners Whin. For a small outlay of approximately £70,000—as part of a local

works at Shaftholme, Aycliffe and Relly Mill. Apart from the speed benefit for Inter-City trains, some of this work was part of local rationalisation plans with additional financial savings.

When work was completed—for the start of the 1970 timetable—the following seven sections of route were authorised for 95/100 m.p.h.; Woolmer Green–Holme (45 miles), Peterborough (Spittal)–Newark South (42), Newark North–Egmanton (8), Retford–Bawtry (8), Doncaster–Selby (17), Barlby–York (Chaloners Whin) (10), York

A panoramic view of the 80 ft. long signalling control panel at King's Cross, which covers the movement of all trains over 83½ route miles of busy railway.

Inset left: The station announcer, who has a full view of train movements depicted by colour lights on the panel, broadcasts the latest information on arrivals and departures.

Inset right: Push buttons change both points and signals to set up complete routes for approaching trains.

Massive track re-alignments enabled the Deltics to reach their full potential, and paved the way for Inter-City 125 trains. A recent civil engineering task was the re-modelling of the approach to King's Cross, through Copenhagen and Gasworks tunnels, known as 'The Throat'. This had been a notorious bottleneck for years because of conflicting Main Line and local train movements.

rationalisation scheme—it was possible to raise the speed on both sides of Selby from 45/50 to 60/80 m.p.h., though there remains a severe restriction over the swing bridge. The final section of route upgraded at this stage was the 36 miles between Darlington and Newcastle. Hitherto, only four miles had been suitable for 100 m.p.h. but this was raised to 15, and increases in speed at lower levels were made at several other places. This involved realignment of curves, strengthening of track and minor bridgework and gave the following line speed improvements:—Bradbury (80 to 100 m.p.h.), north of Ferryhill (80 to 90/100), Browney (70 to 80),

Durham (50 to 70), Chester-le-Street to Tyne Yard (90 to 100) and north of Tyne Yard (35/55 to 55/75 m.p.h.). Following resignalling at Darlington and Ferryhill, line speeds at these places were raised from 80 to 100 m.p.h.

Stage Two was completed for the start of the May 1973 timetable. Over 80 per cent of the route between King's Cross and Newcastle had now been brought up to 100 m.p.h. capability to match the Deltic's speed potential. The fastest time between Newcastle and King's Cross was reduced to 3½ hours and to 5½ hours between Edinburgh and King's Cross.

# Deltic zenith

From 1970 to 1974 was a period of solid
progress in the long-term development of the East
Coast Inter-City business. Completion of line speed
improvements and delivery of new Mark II stock
helped B.R. maintain growth in their business.
Traffic increased—particularly Anglo-Scottish—
and additional services were provided
to meet passenger demand. The increase in
Anglo-Scottish custom was partly due to the
impact of North Sea oil activity. Additional trains
were added to the King's Cross, Newcastle,
Edinburgh and Aberdeen service. A package of
improvements introduced in 1972 provided for
acceleration of the daytime King's Cross–Aberdeen
service by 36 minutes to reach Aberdeen in 9 hr.
9 min., additional Deltic-plus-eight trains between
King's Cross and Newcastle, and a new later
evening service at 19.00 for King's Cross to
Newcastle. An enhanced service of four trains each
way was also introduced between King's Cross,
Lincoln and South Humberside to meet a potential
market. As already mentioned, a general
acceleration of East Coast services followed in 1973
giving fastest times from King's Cross of 2hr. 28 min.
to Leeds, 3½ hr. to Newcastle and 5½ hr. to
Edinburgh. A 116 minute timing for the 07.45
King's Cross–Newcastle Deltic-plus-eight train over
the 160½ miles from Stevenage to York gave the
East Coast Route its first 83 m.p.h. booking. The
14.00 from King's Cross was extended from
Edinburgh to Aberdeen, with a new southbound
service at 09.00. Stevenage station, rebuilt on a new
location, was opened up as an Inter-City railhead.
Two more services were provided for Edinburgh
passengers in 1975—the 07.45 Deltic-plus-eight
train from King's Cross to Newcastle was extended
to Edinburgh, with a return train at 14.50 from
Edinburgh to King's Cross, and new departures at
17.00 from both King's Cross and Edinburgh were
introduced.

Compared with the five trains each way
between King's Cross and Edinburgh in the 1962
timetable, the service today comprises a total of

nine northbound and 10 southbound trains. The service between King's Cross and the West Riding and Hull has also been increased over the years. Although additional sets were allocated to the route as business increased most of the extra services have been covered by more productive use of existing sets. A case in point was the additional King's Cross–Newcastle services introduced in 1972 where two sets of stock were rostered for three separate trips between King's Cross and Newcastle, totalling 805 miles of daily high-speed work.

A range of departures throughout the day between 07.30 and 19.00 gives the train planners the opportunity to programme additional work for the route's fleet of trains. For example, the 08.45 from Aberdeen to King's Cross, arriving at 17.53, returns north as the 19.05 to York; on the following morning the set leaves York as the 08.05 for King's Cross, where it then forms the 12.15 King's Cross to Aberdeen. The two sets each cover 712 miles a day. Other sets work daily rosters involving Leeds–Edinburgh–King's Cross–Leeds or Newcastle–Edinburgh–King's Cross–Newcastle. The much longer journey times operating in steam days precluded this level of daily utilisation.

Although commercially gratifying, the increase in the number of trains on the East Coast Route created a complex operating situation. Three main problems—the availability of Deltic locomotives, signalling in the London area and platform capacity at King's Cross—has inhibited full development of the service in recent years. While 22 Deltics were sufficient to meet the level of business in 1962 this is no longer so 15 years later when the number of trains necessary to cope with today's traffic has—because the Deltics are fully utilised—made it necessary to use Class 47 locomotives for more than half of the trains in today's timetable. While all daytime trains out of Euston can be timed on similar loads with Class 87 power at equal speeds, the East Coast Route—

A Deltic secondman's view of the southern approach to Selby swing-bridge, in May 1969.

because of the differences in point-to-point running times for Deltic and Class 47 locomotives—has been unable to maintain a standard departure pattern from King's Cross to the West Riding or from Edinburgh to King's Cross. To cope with the problem of varying timing-loads, and the pattern of intermediate stops, a number of trains—to get the best use of line capacity between King's Cross and Doncaster—run in groups. The 15.55 Deltic-plus-eight for Leeds, the 16.00 for Edinburgh (Deltic 385 tons), and the 16.05 Bradford (Class 47-plus-eight) are typical of this type of planning; further groupings are at 17.00, 17.04 and 17.10 and at 18.00, 18.04 and 18.08. The Up *"Hull Pullman"*, *"Leeds Executive"* and *"Bradford Executive"* due in King's Cross at 09.55, 10.00 and 10.08 form a group of 100 m.p.h. timed trains at a close headway from Doncaster to King's Cross. In some cases special arrangements have been made to position Deltics to cover certain trains. To cope with the business generated by the 06.45 *"Hull Pullman"*, an additional coach was added to the formation, but this exceeded the timing-load for a Class 47. In this case a Deltic was provided off an Up overnight train from Edinburgh to King's Cross, detached at Doncaster and worked to Hull for the Pullman.

Train service developments on other routes have also affected the timing of East Coast trains—to find a path for the northbound and southbound Edinburgh–Plymouth trains, the southbound *"Flying Scotsman"* now leaves Edinburgh at 09.50 and the northbound *"Aberdonian"* leaves King's Cross at 12.15 instead of 12.00. Fortunately, with completion of resignalling of the main line from Sandy to King's Cross and remodelling of the terminal layout at King's Cross, the capacity problems have now been resolved.

Deltic No. 9001 "Pinza" on the 12.00 Edinburgh to King's Cross near Penmanshiel in 1972.

# Final years

Two major problems affecting the East Coast Route during the final years of the Deltic Era have been the impact of the economic recession and engineering work on the route in preparation for "Inter-City 125" trains. As the effects of the economic crisis began to bite, passenger business on Inter-City trains started to decline; both first and second class loadings were affected. Lower levels of industrial activity reduced the need for business executive travel and the lower levels of disposable income reduced the scope for optional or pleasure travel. There was also considerable market resistance to the impact of fare increases during 1975 and 1976. These had to be raised to a level well beyond what the market could absorb, following the Government's new policy on nationalised industry subsidies. The sector of the East Coast market to be worst hit was the London–West Riding service, to the extent that some trains were withdrawn in May 1976. Anglo-Scottish business, although reduced, was not affected to the same extent.

There are welcome signs that the worst effects of the recession on East Coast Route business have now been passed. As is always the case in any railway modernisation the situation has to get worse before it can get better. This has been the case for daytime Anglo-Scottish trains for the two timetable years of 1975 and 1976. To cope with pre-engineering work for Inter-City 125 services, it was necessary to have single line working between 08.00 and 16.00 on Mondays to Fridays between Berwick and Edinburgh. Most daytime trains had about 15 minutes added to their schedules. However, this work is now complete and the *"Flying Scotsman"* timing has been restored, and, in fact, cut by a few minutes to 5 hr. 27 min.—fastest in its history. The 15.00 Edinburgh–King's Cross, despite three stops, of which the one at Newcastle is extended to eight minutes, now completes the journey in 5 hr. 36 min.

In any aspect of life, progress is inevitably tinged with nostalgia. In the same way that Deltics

displaced the steam giants of the past the Inter-City 125 sets will now displace the Deltics. But one should not forget that much of what will be possible in the next era has been pioneered by the 15 years of the Deltic Era.

## Silver Jubilee

An appropriate bridge between the past, the present and the future was created by the Eastern Region in June 1977 with the introduction between the Scottish and English capitals of the *"Silver Jubilee"* express, a modern counterpart of the famous streamliner of the Thirties. At the head of the train was, fittingly, a mighty Deltic bearing the train's name on a special headboard.

Along the length of the train, colourful destination labels repeated the message that the *"Silver Jubilee"* express was back on Britain's rails. Passengers were assisted by staff wearing *"Silver Jubilee"* lapel badges and travel tickets were issued in a commemorative ticket wallet.

The focal point of the train was the buffet car where, along with the usual catering service by Travellers-Fare, passengers were able to absorb railway history in words and pictures in a unique mobile exhibition.

In order to celebrate Her Majesty the Queen's Silver Jubilee and to commemorate the long association of the East Coast Main Line with journeys made by the Royal Family, the specially decorated buffet featured:–Royalty and the railways, the past 25 years of railways, reproductions of original *"Silver Jubilee"* publicity material and record breakers on the railways.

The Deltic Era is approaching twilight days but let it be remembered for what it was and still is—a glorious chapter in a railway story which has no real ending. The next chapter of that story will be ushered in by Inter-City 125.

Tomorrow's souvenirs! Some of the items produced for the "Silver Jubilee" train in 1977 – menu cards, ticket wallets, seat headrests, serviettes and coffee cup 'sleeves'.

Moment of glory for Deltic No. 55012 "Crepello" at Darlington on the inaugural run of the "Silver Jubilee" – a famous train name of the past revived in June 1977 as part of a year of celebrations.

# Towards Tomorrow

By W. A. Porter,
Assistant Public Relations Officer, British Rail, Eastern Region

Breathless hush of a summer day
. . . shimmering rails converging in infinity . . .
the lazy buzzing of a sated bumble-bee in lineside knapweed,
the muted chatter of a tractor on a distant farm.

Silence in the sun.

Far off, a celandine speck in the quivering haze
. . . a distant hum of steel wheel upon steel rail
. . . a sudden whine,
a blur of gold – and blue – and white
– a rush in the air as tall grasses lean back in submission . . .
a flash of colour, like the startled kingfisher
as he flees his river's edge,
gone in a moment like a dart in flight . . .

To observe the passage of Inter-City 125, British Rail's new thoroughbred, is to savour fresh dimensions in high speed and muffled sound. To travel in its armchair air-conditioned comfort is to experience an exciting new chapter in rail travel.

Very soon these thoroughbreds of tomorrow, ranking with the swiftest and most comfortable trains in the world, will bridge astonishing new frontiers in rail travel between London, Yorkshire, the North-east and Scotland. They will reach 125 m.p.h. over long stretches of the East Coast Main Line – the scene of so many of yesteryear's splendid railway achievements – which railway engineers are fitting out for the High Speed Era. Previous limits in the realms of speed will become dim memories as Inter-City 125 flashes into this last quarter of the Twentieth Century.

By 1979 journeys of just over three hours between London and Newcastle – 268 miles at an average speed of about 85 m.p.h. – will be commonplace. One train, the *"Flying Scotsman"*, will cover the distance at an average speed of 90 m.p.h. New multi-aspect colour-light signals giving train crews much more information about conditions on the track ahead of them, simplified

and improved track layouts and the removal of historical bottlenecks on what was for many years the "Blue Riband" railway route in Britain, are creating a rail clearway through the Eastern half of the country.

Imagine . . . . . it will soon be possible to set out from London King's Cross and reach Doncaster, 156 miles away, in just 99 minutes at an average speed of 94.5 m.p.h. – 25 minutes and 19 m.p.h. faster than today.

A 4½-hour journey from London to Edinburgh – an hour faster than the fastest today by the *"Flying Scotsman"* – will reflect an average running speed of over 87 m.p.h. for the 393 miles between the capitals. Starting in May 1978, the 10.00 hours *"Flying Scotsman"* will run non-stop from King's Cross to Newcastle in 183 minutes at an

The first Eastern Region 'Inter-City 125' production set 254 001 heads north from York on a proving run in September 1977.

average speed of almost 88 m.p.h. Arrival in Edinburgh will be at 14.50 in 290 minutes from King's Cross, giving an overall average of 81.31 m.p.h. Track improvements between Newcastle and Edinburgh will clip almost another ten minutes off this section by May 1979, when "Oil City" Aberdeen, 523 miles from London, will be reached in 7 hours 20 minutes instead of the present 9 hours 7 minutes.

No wheels in modern transport, other than steel upon steel, will cover such long distances so speedily, so safely, so comfortably, so conveniently or so reliably.

The new generation of sleek lightweight trains, an adroit extension of existing rail technology typifying the best in British engineering, will enter commercial service on Eastern Region early in 1978. During the first few months they will run at existing timings. In May, however, there will be a limited speed-up and full scale accelerations will take place in May 1979 when the whole fleet of 32 on order for the East Coast Main Line becomes available. Maximum potential on the Anglo-Scottish run will be reached in 1980 when re-signalling in the Doncaster area is completed.

By then York will be half-an-hour closer to London in just over two hours travel averaging 91 m.p.h., and the 186 miles between London and Leeds will also be covered in slightly over two hours at 86 m.p.h. Bradford, too, will be 30 minutes closer to the capital in just 2½ hours.

The 232 miles that separate London and Darlington will be run at an average of 92 m.p.h. to slash 28 minutes from the present three-hour journey. Here are some examples of the dramatic cuts in journey times which will be effected by Inter-City 125 trains:

| London to— | 1977/78 | 1979/80 |
|---|---|---|
| Edinburgh | 5hr. 27m. | 4hr. 30m. |
| Newcastle | 3hr. 33m. | 2hr. 55m. |
| Darlington | 2hr. 59m. | 2hr. 31m. |
| York | 2hr. 31m. | 2hr. 04m. |
| Leeds | 2hr. 30m. | 2hr. 09m. |
| Wakefield | 2hr. 14m. | 1hr. 53m. |
| Doncaster | 2hr. 05m. | 1hr. 39m. |
| Peterborough | 1hr. 00m. | 0hr. 49m. |

Improved train speeds on the East Coast Main Line achieved by signalling and engineering projects.

| | Line speeds before improvements |
|---|---|
| | 1977 line speeds |
| | Planned works |

King's Cross · Welwyn Garden City · Hitchin · Huntingdon · Peterborough · Grantham · Newark · Retford · Doncaster · Selby · York

| 80 | 90 | 90 | 100 | 70 | 20 | 100 | 70 | 60 | 80 | 60 | 45 | 25 | 100 |
|---|---|---|---|---|---|---|---|---|---|---|---|---|---|
| 100 | 100 | 100 | 100 | 100 | 100 | 100 | 100 | 85 | | 80 | 60 | 40 | 25 | 100 |
| 105 | 125 | 125 | 125 | 125 | 105 | 125 | 100 | 125 | 115 | 125 | 105 | 40 | 25 | 125 |

Distance in miles from King's Cross.  50m    100m    150m    188m

| Darlington | Durham | | Newcastle | Morpeth | Alnmouth | Belford | Berwick | | Dunbar | | Edinburgh |
|---|---|---|---|---|---|---|---|---|---|---|---|
| 80 | 35 | 80 | 15 | 40 | 60 | 90 | 30 | 75 | 60 | 75 | |
| 100 | 75 | 90 | 15 | 40 | 60 | 100 | 80 | 80 | 60 | 80 | |
| 125 | 75 | 110 | 15 | 50 | 80 | 125 | 80 | 85 | 80 | 100 | |

250m      300m      350m      393m

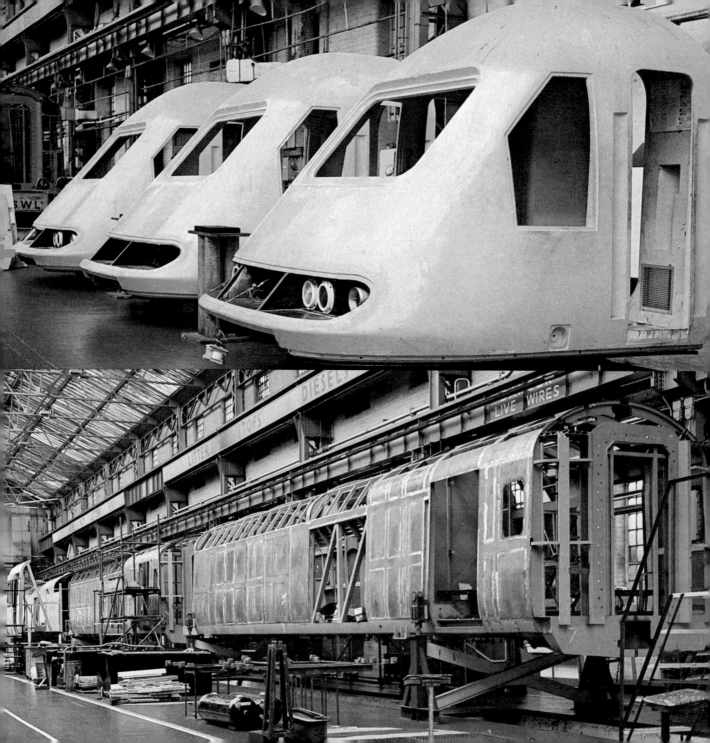

# Preparing a way . . . . .

In ideal circumstances all the Inter-City 125 fliers would have been introduced to the East Coast Main Line at one stroke but this would have been to disregard the realities of cut-backs in investment and the need to take advantage of the available investment as quickly as possible.

Even in the late Sixties only 95 miles of the East Coast Main Line – not even one-quarter of the distance between the capitals of England and Scotland – were fit for 100 m.p.h. running. Massive line engineering schemes, now entering their final stages, were embarked upon at the turn of the decade. By 1970 the track mileage for 100 m.p.h. running had risen to 170 miles. By 1973 it was 210 miles.

Engineering objectives in the early Seventies included elimination of the worst and most notorious bottleneck of all on the East Coast Route, at Peterborough, where the old Railway Companies layouts restricted trains to 20 m.p.h. Now, through trains negotiate Peterborough at 100 m.p.h., and new track layouts and associated improvements have extended the mileage over which trains can run at this speed to over 240 of the 268 miles between London and Newcastle.

The old semaphore signals are passing into history too, and in a few years only five major signalboxes equipped with the very latest in electronics will control the whole of the East Coast Route to Newcastle. The new power-operated signalling centre at King's Cross, completed in April 1977 with the end of the station ''Throat'' works – a virtual rebuilding of the approaches to this important terminus – and a new signalbox at Peterborough already control 101 miles of the route. Work is proceeding on a new signalbox at Doncaster which will embrace another 84 miles, and the rest of the route will be governed by the modern installations at York and Newcastle, and eventually by a new box at Edinburgh.

In his chapter on the Sixties and early Seventies, Brian Perren has described how track and signalling improvements over the years were matched by more powerful locomotives and modern rolling stock capable of running at higher speeds and providing steady improvements in passenger comfort and amenities. The upper limits of the Deltics performance having been reached, the enhanced potential of track and signalling was there to be exploited. A new form of traction was required to do it.

# The Thoroughbreds . . . . .

The new form of traction is, of course, the Class 254, Inter-City 125 High Speed Train. That these trains will achieve a breakthrough as dramatic as that established by the transition from steam to Deltic power in the early Sixties is without doubt.

In fact, the speed-up from the already fast timings will be even greater in degree. And it will not only be speed but glass-smooth riding, even greater all-round comfort, an entirely new concept in catering and, above all, space to work, to walk about or just to relax – advantages which no other form of transport can equal.

Investigations into the feasibility of running trains at speeds which were hitherto regarded as pipe-dreams were initiated in the Sixties. Other railway administrations, notably the Japanese, constructed specially-designed railway systems at enormous capital cost but British Rail endeavoured to research high speed running on its most valuable asset – the existing railway. Ever-increasing competition from a rapidly expanding network of Motorways and air services decreed that the new railway revolution must take shape quickly. It was therefore decided that the urgent needs of the Seventies would best be met by developing a conventional train capable of running at 125 m.p.h.

To produce a conventional train with this capability required that something fundamental be done about the power/weight ratio. Two power

Glass fibre nose shells (top) for Inter-City 125 Power Cars ready for fitting to the body shells (bottom) at the Crewe Works of British Rail Engineering Ltd.

units were needed to spread weight and reduce engine axle-loading. It was therefore logical to place one at each end of the train, enhancing smoothness in acceleration and deceleration from a passenger viewpoint and enabling the train operator to boost utilisation by avoiding the need to couple and uncouple locomotives at the end of a journey. The provision of two power cars instead of one also greatly improves reliability. It is known, for instance, that Inter-City 125 can keep going at over 100 m.p.h. "on the flat" on one engine only.

Engineers also evolved a new lightweight coach of integral body design which would run at speeds 25 per cent higher than before and incorporate the best features of passenger vehicles produced in the last few years. The 75 feet coach – 10 feet longer than existing vehicles – will also save bogie weight. A train of 10 traditional coaches – 645 feet over 20 bogies – provides no more seats than an eight coach Inter-City 125 set 600 feet over only 16 bogies.

Inter-City 125 is, therefore, a natural step in British Rail's quest for improved journey times. At minimal cost it has been possible to produce a far superior train as the standard Inter-City service. Advanced technology and design have enabled the weight of Inter-City 125 to be reduced by about 25 per cent compared with existing trains of similar capacity.

The cost of the entire project on Eastern Region – this includes provision of 32 train sets, all track and signalling work and the construction of maintenance depots – is about £70 million. A mere 20 miles of Motorway would cost the taxpayer more.

## Customer care . . . . .

Inter-City 125 on Eastern Region will comprise two streamlined diesel-electric power cars, one at each end of the train, and eight of the new 75ft. long Mark III passenger coaches, including catering vehicles. Each power car has a driving cab and is equipped with a Paxman 2,250 h.p. diesel engine with Brush electrical equipment,

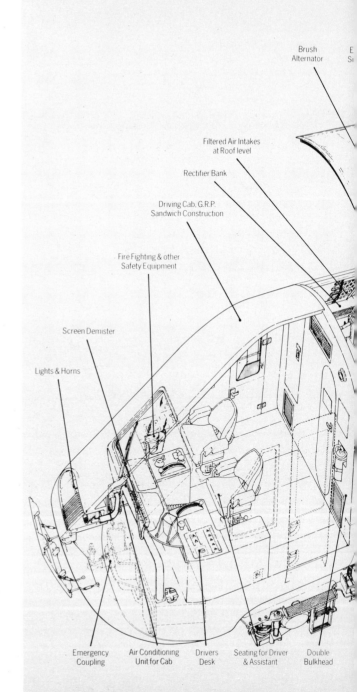

Brush Alternator

Filtered Air Intakes at Roof level

Rectifier Bank

Driving Cab, G.R.P. Sandwich Construction

Fire Fighting & other Safety Equipment

Screen Demister

Lights & Horns

Emergency Coupling

Air Conditioning Unit for Cab

Drivers Desk

Seating for Driver & Assistant

Double Bulkhead

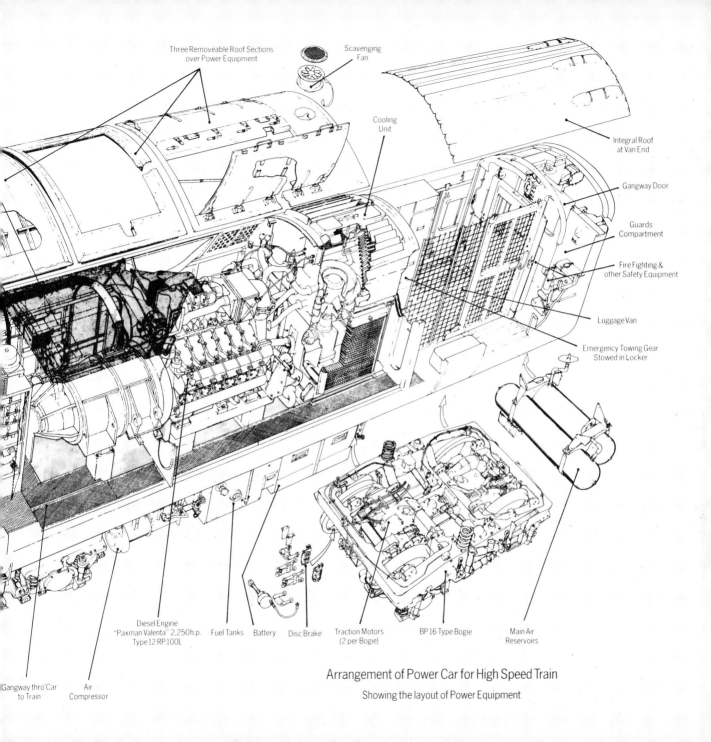

Three Removeable Roof Sections over Power Equipment

Scavenging Fan

Cooling Unit

Integral Roof at Van End

Gangway Door

Guards Compartment

Fire Fighting & other Safety Equipment

Luggage Van

Emergency Towing Gear Stowed in Locker

Gangway thro'Car to Train

Air Compressor

Diesel Engine "Paxman Valenta" 2,250 h.p. Type 12 RP.100L

Fuel Tanks

Battery

Disc Brake

Traction Motors (2 per Bogie)

BP 16 Type Bogie

Main Air Reservoirs

## Arrangement of Power Car for High Speed Train
Showing the layout of Power Equipment

giving a total train output of 4,500 h.p.

The Mark III carriage, of lightweight welded steel construction, has air-sprung disc-braked bogies and is air-conditioned. Interior doors open automatically into a passenger area equipped with ergonomically-designed seating, tinted double-glazed windows and a public address system. First-class saloons have 48 seats and second-class saloons 72 seats. The pleasing decor of the passenger saloons is supplemented by the use of easy-to-clean light-coloured materials for walls and other surfaces while fully-fitted carpets in all vehicles add a touch of luxury. Colourful fabrics have been chosen for the seats, the covers of which can be removed for cleaning or replacement. Generous luggage space is provided between the seats and on shelves above the windows. Bays at the end of each coach permit larger items of luggage to be stowed out of sight. Fluorescent strip lighting behind ceiling diffusers gives an even balance of light throughout the saloons.

Toilets at each end of every coach feature foot-operated controls for both handbasins and WC's and match the high standard of the rest of the passenger accommodation. Getting on and off the train has also been made easier – especially for those carrying cases – by the extra-wide entrance doors.

# Catering concept . . . . .

An entirely new catering concept aboard Inter-City 125 trains represents the first major investment in on-train catering for nearly 20 years. As with passenger saloons, the emphasis in catering vehicles is upon creating a quite new passenger environment more in keeping with the sophisticated demands of the Seventies.

Three entirely new catering vehicles are being built:
* A restaurant/kitchen vehicle which will provide a full meals service.
* A restaurant/buffet vehicle which will provide a modern and comprehensive buffet/snack service throughout the train.

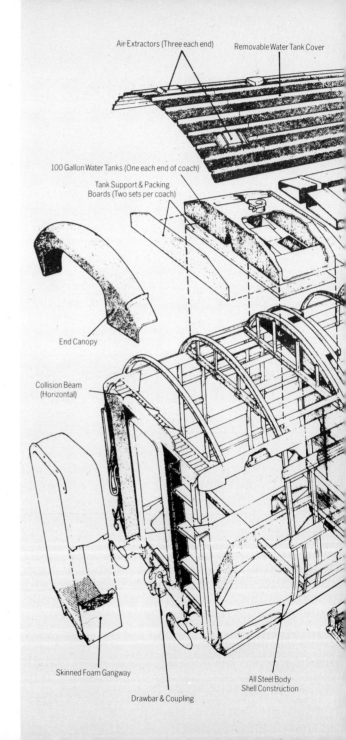

Air Extractors (Three each end)

Removable Water Tank Cover

100 Gallon Water Tanks (One each end of coach)

Tank Support & Packing Boards (Two sets per coach)

End Canopy

Collision Beam (Horizontal)

Skinned Foam Gangway

Drawbar & Coupling

All Steel Body Shell Construction

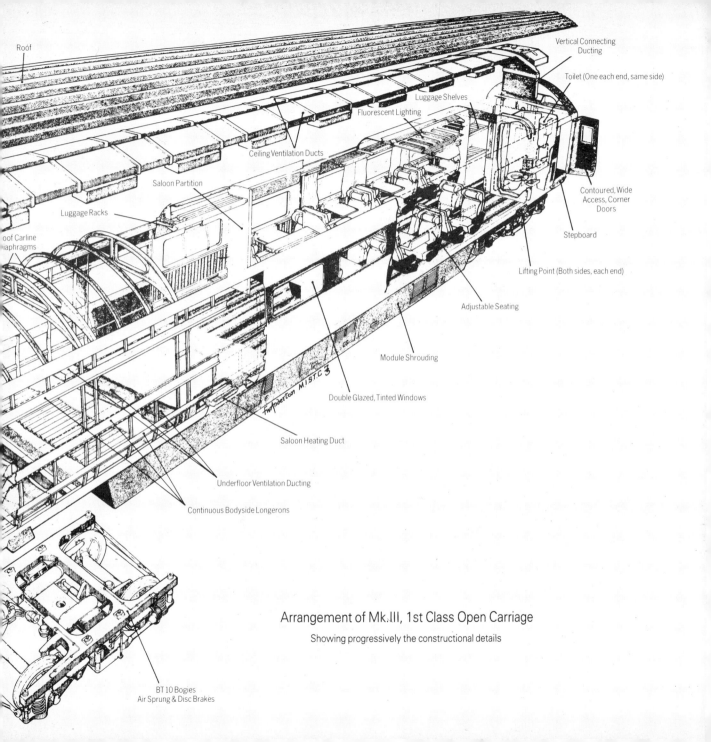

Roof

Ceiling Ventilation Ducts

Saloon Partition

Luggage Racks

oof Carline
iaphragms

Vertical Connecting
Ducting

Toilet (One each end, same side)

Luggage Shelves

Fluorescent Lighting

Contoured, Wide
Access, Corner
Doors

Stepboard

Lifting Point (Both sides, each end)

Adjustable Seating

Module Shrouding

Double Glazed, Tinted Windows

Saloon Heating Duct

Underfloor Ventilation Ducting

Continuous Bodyside Longerons

BT 10 Bogies
Air Sprung & Disc Brakes

fwhaerton M1STC 3

### Arrangement of Mk.III, 1st Class Open Carriage
Showing progressively the constructional details

\* A restaurant/buffet vehicle which will combine the buffet/snack facility with a full meals service.

These amenities will be supplemented by gangway trolleys which will bring hot and cold drinks, sandwiches and snacks right to the passenger's seat. The buffet services will include a selection of hot meals like bacon and eggs, pizzas, toasted sandwiches or steaklets – cooked to order by microaire oven – which the customer can take back to his seat in specially-designed trays. There will be a full meals service to first-class passengers at their seats.

Thirst quenchers will include draught beer or lager and a wide range of short drinks in miniature bottles which can be enjoyed in the social area at the end of the buffet car where the decor of flame red panelling creates a warm, relaxed atmosphere. Eastern Region will receive 52 catering vehicles. Restaurant and buffet vehicles will work together in 20 designated sets which will be allocated to the Anglo-Scottish services and principal business trains to and from the Provinces.

## Eastern promise . . . . .

The new trains will not only be much faster, more comfortable and more reliable than ever before. There will be more of them and more train seats between the places they serve. And routes which are not at present earmarked for Inter-City 125, will not become rail "Cinderellas" as they will derive immediate benefit from the "cascade" effect of modern air-conditioned coaching stock displaced on primary routes by Inter-City 125. Notable among these will be the East Anglian services linking London with Ipswich and Norwich. Even as this book went to press, a case for additional Inter-City sets for Eastern Region use was under way.

With Inter-City 125 there will be hourly trains between the Scottish and English capitals, providing limited stops on the even hour and calls on the odd hour at York, Darlington, Newcastle and Berwick. The 19 trains now linking Edinburgh and London daily will be increased to 22 (11 in each direction).

Newcastle, at present served daily by 14 trains to London and 15 from London, will have 18 in each direction. Darlington will have 17 to London and 16 from London (11 to London and 13 from London at present). York will have 37 train connections with London (19 to London and 18 from London) – nine more than now. Peterborough will receive 50 trains a day – ten more than the existing 20 in each direction.

West Yorkshire, industrial heart of Eastern Region will, apart from the non-stop *"Leeds Executive"*, enjoy an hourly service from Leeds to London with stops at Wakefield, Doncaster and Peterborough or at Wakefield only. In this area too, the number of services will be boosted. Leeds and Wakefield will both have 26 services (13 in each direction) instead of 22, and Doncaster's existing 39 will be boosted to 50. Most stations south of Doncaster will have a two-hourly main line service calling at intermediate points from Huntingdon, though these will be provided by fast conventional train sets.

More trains will, of course, mean a wider choice of seats for Inter-City travellers – 1,000 more each day between Edinburgh and London (9,200

This trolley service brings hot and cold drinks, sandwiches and snacks right to the passenger's seat. It is part of the new catering concept on the Inter-City 125 trains which includes meals cooked to order by microaire oven.

instead of 8,200); 4,400 more between Newcastle and London (16,100 instead of 11,700); 4,000 more between Leeds and London (11,700 instead of 7,700).

Inter-City 125 will also add useful hours to the time at a businessman's disposal for face-to-face meetings with clients and colleagues. It will be possible to arrive earlier and to leave later, yet not spend additional time away from home. The new thoroughbreds should provide British Rail with a powerful answer to air and long-distance road competition by meeting customer requirements for fast regular services with minimum end-to-end journey times. A 30 per cent increase in railway earnings is expected in the first three years.

After crew training, the first four Inter-City 125 trains will be introduced into conventional services on the East Coast Main Line early in 1978. Then, in May 1978, as more units are delivered from B.R.E.L. Works and as the Region breaks free of the shackles placed upon high speed running by vital engineering works on the line, an interim timetable will come into operation, employing eight sets on accelerated timings. Further units will be introduced during the year until the full squadron of 32 "fliers" is available in May 1979.

## All Systems Go . . . . .

Throughout the history of railways, safety has played a dominant role in determining the type of service to be offered to the customer. Improved braking techniques on the new thoroughbreds, combined with the new colour-light signalling system are designed to maintain British Rail's enviable safety record.

Where lines have been upgraded, including the provision of continuous welded rails, to cater for the higher speeds, signals have been respaced to provide the braking distances necessary at the higher speeds. The signals will, therefore, continue to present clear and simple messages to the driver and ensure safe operation at the higher speeds. As

a back-up to the signals seen by the driver is the Automatic Warning System which rings a bell on the footplate for a green signal, sounds an alarm for yellow and red signals. It also applies the brakes unless the driver acknowledges the warning by pressing an acceptance button, when, as a reminder, it reinforces the warning with a black and yellow display on a visual indicator.

The signalling system makes a vital contribution to safe running of trains at 125 m.p.h. or any speed up to that figure.

## The Record Breakers . . . . .

It seemed as if the heatwave would never end. It was yet another day for shirt-sleeves and the shade.

In the welcoming cool beneath the high arches of York station, drama was in the making as Driver Jim Wilson released the brakes on his sleek new train.

It was 09.34 on Tuesday 12 June 1973. The daily dramas that are the fabric of any large railway station were to be dwarfed on this warm morning as Jim and his "second man", Roland Wilson, eased the long streamlined train out over the points and crossings of the busy main-line station.

It was the day when a world record was to be made – twice!

Just three miles out, with the needle passing the 75 m.p.h. mark, the prototype of British Rail's High Speed Train was accelerating smoothly and quietly. Five miles out and doing the "ton" . . . . ten miles out and already eclipsing the world steam speed record of 126 m.p.h. claimed before the war by *"Mallard"*, the shimmering blue steam veteran now nestling in the National Railway Museum at York.

Twelve miles out and passing 130 . . . . past milepost 21 and hitting 140 . . . . through Thirsk station and out into open country again . . . . 143 miles-an-hour . . . . a mile in 25 seconds . . . . a new world record for diesel trains and the fastest train

The sleek, modern bar on each Inter-City 125 train even serves draught bitter.

ever to run in Britain.

In fact, the precursor of Inter-City 125 had reached 143.2 m.p.h. at milepost 25¼ on that unforgettable run. A log of the run is reproduced on page 84.

The train make-up included two power cars, two non-standard vehicles (a test car and a Mark II Buffet Car), and three Mark III coaches, one of which had been converted for use as a temporary test car by removal of most of the seats and installation of electronic recording equipment operated by staff from the Railway Technical Centre, Derby. The record-breaking run was part of a series of tests authorised by the Chief Mechanical and Electrical Engineer, British Railways Board, to establish the power car performance and the riding, braking and air-conditioning properties of the new train. They were carried out jointly by the Testing and Performance and Power Equipment Sections of the C.M.&.E.E. Department. The Research and Development Divisions also participated, to obtain data relative to high speed running, for Advanced Passenger Train design purposes.

The new world record was in fact repeated just two hours later on a second high-speed run between York and Darlington which was even more spectacular than the first, with the train maintaining an average speed in excess of 140 m.p.h. over a distance of 12 miles. The train again

reached 143.2 m.p.h., this time at milepost 28, and a brake-stop from 139.5 m.p.h. at milepost 35 saw the train brought to a stand in 2,392 yards (72 seconds). A log of this run is reproduced on page 85.

It had been a week of high drama for railwaymen the country over, especially so in "Railway City" York. For the cracking pace set by the new train during 120,000 miles of exhaustive test running, much of it on the "racetrack" between York and Darlington, approached a crescendo on 6 June when the prototype broke the 35-year-old world steam speed record by running at 131 m.p.h. Driver Ernest Cockerham was later quoted as saying: "It handled as easily as an expensive motor car. When we slowed down to 90 miles-an-hour you felt you could step out of the cab and walk".

Just five days later, with 54-year-old York driver Sidney Winfield and David Jameson (40) of Leeds as "second man", the prototype reached 141 m.p.h. over a one mile stretch (between mileposts 18 and 17) on a southbound run from Darlington to York. This was eight m.p.h. faster than the world diesel speed record established in 1939 by Germany's *Flying Hamburger*. On the northbound run speeds of 130 m.p.h. and above had been sustained for 22 miles between mileposts 16 and 38, with a maximum of 139 m.p.h. at milepost 34. Driver Winfield was instructed at Darlington to attempt to exceed 140 m.p.h. on the return run.

12 June 1973 – the prototype High Speed Train flashes past the camera and breaks two speed records at the same time.

# Prototype High Speed Train journey log

| | | | |
|---|---|---|---|
| Date | 12 JUNE 1973 | Journey | YORK – DARLINGTON |
| Train formation | 2 POWER CARS AND 6 COACHES | Weather | FINE AND DRY |

| Time | Location | M.P.H. | Remarks |
|---|---|---|---|
| 09·34·00 | York | 0 | Depart |
| 37·34 | MP 1 | 46·5 | |
| 38·49 | MP 2 | 18·0 | Start of Acceleration |
| 39·18 | MP 3 | 68·25 | |
| 42·02 | MP 4 | 89·2 | |
| 42·39 | MP 5 | 99·7 | |
| | Beningbrough | | |
| 43·13 | MP 6 | 104·2 | |
| 43·45 | MP 7 | 114·7 | |
| 44·16 | MP 8 | 120·4 | |
| 44·43 | MP 9 | 124·2 | |
| | Tollerton | | |
| 45·14 | MP 10 | 127·1 | |
| 45·42 | MP 11 — Alne | 130·5 | |
| 46·09 | MP 12 | 129 | |
| 46·36 | MP 13 | 130·5 | |
| | Raskelf | | |
| 47·05 | MP 14 | 129 | |
| 47·32 | MP 15 | 132·7 | |
| | Pilmoor | | |
| 47·59 | MP 16 | 135 | |
| 48·26 | MP 17 | 135 | |
| 48·52 | MP 18 — Sessay | 137·7 | |
| 49·19 | MP 19 | 138 | |
| 49·45 | MP 20 | 138·7 | |
| 50·11 | MP 21 | 141 | |
| | Thirsk | | |
| 50·36 | MP 22 | 141·75 | |
| 51·02 | MP 23 | 141·75 | |
| 51·27 | MP 24 | 141 | No great impression of speed. |
| 51·53 | MP 25 | 141 | Noise level very acceptable. |
| 52·18 | MP 26 — Otterington | 141 | Attained 143·2 at mile post 25½. |
| 52·44 | MP 27 | 138 | Maximum Speed Power Off. |
| 53·11 | MP 28 | 129 | Riding very smooth and quiet. |
| | MP 29 | | |
| | MP 30 — Northallerton | | Coast down to Darlington. Arr. Darlington 10·04·24 |
| | MP 31 | | |
| | MP 32 | | |
| | MP 33 | | |
| | Danby Wiske | | |
| | MP 34 | | |
| | MP 35 | | |
| | MP 36 | | |
| | MP 37 — Cowton | | |
| | MP 38 | | |
| | MP 39 | | |
| | MP 40 | | |
| | MP 41 | | |
| | MP 42 | | |
| | MP 43 | | |
| | MP 44 | | |
| | Darlington | | |

The fastest men on British Rail – for a few days – Drivers Jack Birdsall and Ernest Cockerham, being congratulated by Deputy General Manager, Robert Reid; and Chief Mechanical and Electrical Engineer, Colin Scutt, on 6 June 1973 after breaking "Mallard's" record.

# Prototype High Speed Train journey log

Date __12 JUNE 1973__    Journey __YORK - DARLINGTON__
Train formation __2 POWER CARS AND 5 COACHES__    Weather __FINE AND DRY__

| Time | Location | M.P.H. | Remarks |
|---|---|---|---|
| 11.19.00 | York | 0 | Depart |
| 22.11 | MP 1 | 24 | Start of Acceleration |
| 23.50 | MP 2 | 66 | |
| 24.34 | MP 3 | 86.2 | |
| 25.12 | MP 4 | 99 | |
| 25.47 | MP 5 | 107.2 | |
| | Beningbrough | | |
| 26.19 | MP 6 | 113.2 | |
| 26.50 | MP 7 | 118.9 | |
| 27.19 | MP 8 | 123 | |
| 27.49 | MP 9 | 126 | |
| | Tollerton | | |
| 28.17 | MP 10 | 129 | |
| 28.44 | MP 11 — Alne | 129.8 | |
| 29.12 | MP 12 | 132 | |
| 29.39 | MP 13 | 131.9 | |
| | Raskelf | | |
| 30.07 | MP 14 | 130.5 | |
| 30.34 | MP 15 | 130.9 | |
| | Pilmoor | | |
| 31.02 | MP 16 | 133.5 | |
| 31.28 | MP 17 | 134.2 | |
| 31.55 | MP 18 — Sessay | 136.5 | |
| 32.21 | MP 19 | 137.6 | |
| 32.47 | MP 20 | 138 | |
| 33.13 | MP 21 | 138.8 | |
| | Thirsk | | |
| 11.33.39 | MP 22 | 140.2 | |
| 34.05 | MP 23 | 141 | |
| 34.30 | MP 24 | 141 | |
| 34.56 | MP 25 | 139.9 | |
| 35.22 | MP 26 — Otterington | 140.6 | |
| 35.47 | MP 27 | 140.6 | |
| 36.13 | MP 28 | 143.2 | Max Speed |
| 36.38 | MP 29 | 141 | |
| 37.04 | MP 30 — Northallerton | 139.1 | |
| 37.29 | MP 31 | 142.5 | |
| 37.55 | MP 32 | 141.75 | |
| 38.21 | MP 33 | 141 | |
| | Danby Wiske | | |
| 38.46 | MP 34 | 141 | |
| 39.12 | MP 35 | 139.5 | High Speed brake stop from |
| 39.44 | MP 36 | 84.2 | 139.5 mile/h to 0 in 2392 yds |
| 42.21 | MP 37 — Cowton | 52.5 | Time 11.40.24. |
| 43.13 | MP 38 | 79.5 | |
| 43.55 | MP 39 | 93 | |
| 44.37 | MP 40 | 100.5 | |
| 45.07 | MP 41 | 99 | |
| 45.44 | MP 42 | 91.5 | |
| 46.33 | MP 43 | 55.5 | |
| 48.37 | MP 44 | 15 | |
| 49.00 | Darlington | 0 | Arrive Darlington |

The Control panel, seen from behind the driver's chair (left) of the Inter-City 125 production train. Prototype control panel (top right) and inboard end of the Paxman Valenta power unit (bottom right).

1. Automatic Warning System indicator unit
2. Inspection lamp socket
3. Pressure gauge main reservoir and main reservoir pipe
4. Pressure gauge bogies 1 & 2 brake cylinders
5. Pressure gauge brake pipe
6. Windscreen wiper and washer control
7. Train supply "OFF"
8. Train supply indicator
9. Train supply "ON"
10. Brake overcharge
11. Brake test switch
12. Cab air-conditioning "LOW/HIGH"
13. Parking brake "OFF"
14. Parking brake indicator
15. Parking brake "ON"
16. Fire alarm test
17. Automatic Warning System "IN/OUT" indicator
18. General "Fault" indicator
19. Emergency brake button
20. Brake controller
21. Light switch panel
22. Windscreen washer tank filler
23. Automatic Warning System Yodelarm
24. Notice clip
25. Driver/Guard "bleep"
26. Speedometer
27. Ammeter
28. Clock
29. Wheel slip indicator
30. Engines "STOPPED/RUNNING" indicator

31. Engines "STOP"
32. Driver/Guard button
33. Engines "START"
34. Power controller
35. Driver's selector handle
36. Automatic Warning System re-set button
37. Horn switch
38. Driver/Guard communication handset
39. Fire pull handle
40. Cab air-conditioning vent

Subsequent examination of the instruments aboard the train revealed that it had maintained an average of 140 m.p.h. over a distance of 10¾ miles from milepost 26 to milepost 15¼.

Driver Winfield said: "The train went so smoothly I could have rolled a cigarette or written a letter. I would have gone to 150 m.p.h. if they had let me." Design Engineer for the prototype, Mr. Bruce Sephton, was phlegmatic: "We are not out to break records. We wish to establish an adequate margin for the normal operating speed of 125 miles-an-hour."

Logs of the two runs on 11 June were recorded by Mr. Alan Burrows, then Eastern Region's Project Manager for the train. They are:

| NORTHBOUND | | | SOUTHBOUND | | |
|---|---|---|---|---|---|
| Time | Location | MPH | Time | Location | MPH |
| | MP5 | 105 | | MP39 | 80 |
| 13.28 | MP6 | 113 | | MP38 | 90 |
| | MP8 | 120 | 14.18 | MP37 | 100 |
| 13.29 | MP9 | 124 | | MP36 | 110 |
| 13.31 | MP12 | 129 | | MP35 | 115 |
| | MP15 | 129 | | MP34 | 120 |
| | MP16 | 130 | | MP32 | 125 |
| | MP17 | 131 | | MP31 | 130 |
| | MP18 | 130 | 14.28 pass NORTHALLERTON | | |
| | MP19 | 131 | | MP28 | 133 |
| | MP20 | 131 | | MP27 | 135 |
| | MP21 | 133 | | MP26 | 136 |
| 13.35 pass THIRSK | | | | MP24 | 139 |
| | MP26 | 132 | 14.33 pass THIRSK | | |
| | MP27 | 132 | | MP22 | 138 |
| | MP31 | 134 | | MP20 | 139 |
| | MP33 | 132 | | MP18 | 141 |
| | | 139 | | MP17 | 141 |
| for one mile | | | Then coast down to York | | |
| | MP36 | 134 | | | |
| | MP38 | 130 | | | |
| Full brake application to dead stand 2,160 yards in 68 seconds | | | | | |

It was on the very next day, however, that the 09.34 and the 11.19 out of York raced to 143 miles-an-hour on the stretch of line between Thirsk and Northallerton.

On 3 August the same year, on its first demonstration run, from King's Cross to Darlington and back, Inter-City 125 clocked 135 m.p.h. on the York–Darlington "racetrack". Passengers included Members of Parliament, Trade Union leaders and Journalists. A trial brake stop from 125 m.p.h. to a standstill took 1 mile 260 yards in 57 seconds.

Information gained from the trials and an interim public service which started between Bristol and Paddington on 5 May 1975 was used in the design of the production models; the main external difference from the prototype being an improved front end to the power cars, so giving Inter-City 125 a stronger visual impact.

On 4 October 1976 the world's fastest diesel train service came into operation when a 125 m.p.h. service was introduced on the Paddington–South Wales/Bristol routes. There was an immediate and enthusiastic response from the public. Results by early December showed a 15 per cent increase in business.

## Just around the corner . . . . .

Unlike the crack expresses run in some other countries, usually limited to first-class passengers or with a supplement added to the fare, Inter-City 125 is a train for all at the ordinary or reduced fares without supplement.

There is little doubt that reduced journey time is the most significant individual factor in persuading more passengers to travel by rail. There is abundant proof in history.

But there are limits to the extent to which British Rail can improve train speeds with the present range and style of traction. Inter-City 125 and all the exciting prospects that it brings is not the "end of the line" in British Rail's desire to stay abreast and, indeed, keep ahead of competition.

Scientists at British Rail's Technical Centre

"Fanfare for 001". The official handing over ceremony for Eastern Region's first Inter-City 125 train, on 7 September 1977, was heralded by trumpeters of the Royal Scots Dragoon Guards playing a fanfare specially composed for the occasion.

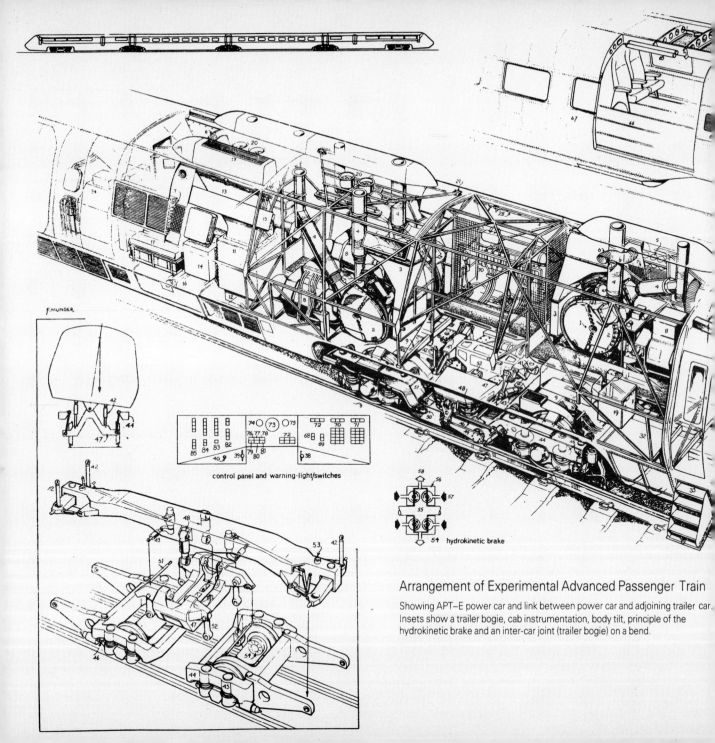

F. MUNGER

control panel and warning-light/switches

hydrokinetic brake

# Arrangement of Experimental Advanced Passenger Train

Showing APT–E power car and link between power car and adjoining trailer car. Insets show a trailer bogie, cab instrumentation, body tilt, principle of the hydrokinetic brake and an inter-car joint (trailer bogie) on a bend.

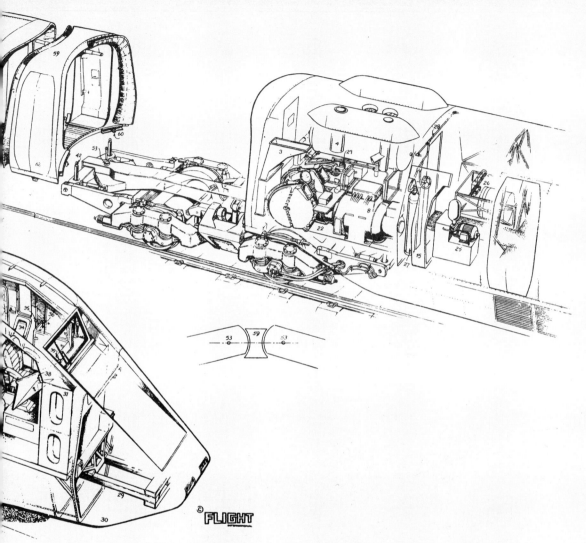

© FLIGHT

in Derby have carried out entirely new research into exploiting to the utmost the potential of guided wheels on steel rails. Much of their efforts concentrated on the behaviour of railway wheels and bogies when cornering, since curves, so predominant on the British railway system, play a major role in inhibiting higher speeds.

The outcome is the development of a new bogie with a unique geometry in its design. Unlike conventional ones, the new design has a self-steering characteristic which places the axles on a radius of a curve, thereby eliminating 'hunting' as a train corners at high speed.

The next problem for the "boffins" was to overcome side forces on the passenger resulting from the train's ability to corner at higher speed. The result of researches was the development of a tilting coach body for greater passenger comfort. This balances centrifugal force, as in an aircraft, so that the passenger rides in much greater comfort. And so the "Advanced Passenger Train" was born.

These new features had to be tested, first experimentally, and then in commercial service. All this was time consuming and it was estimated that a project of such magnitude would take over a decade from drawing board to a comprehensive network of trains running at speeds of around 155 m.p.h.

Inter-City 125, on the other hand, was an extension of existing technology and could be developed more rapidly. It will soon be creating a new high-speed passenger era on Eastern Region but already railwaymen are reaching out towards the next stage. The Advanced Passenger Train programme has continued in parallel with the development of Inter-City 125 and an experimental gas-turbined A.P.T. has already achieved 152 m.p.h. in trial running. Three electric-powered prototypes are being built and will enter

experimental commercial service on the Euston–Glasgow route within the next year or so. Speeds will be limited initially to 125 m.p.h. but will eventually escalate to at least 150 m.p.h.

The lightweight and aerodynamically-shaped A.P.T., embodying the unique suspension system enabling it to negotiate curves in complete safety and with no discomfort to passengers at speeds up to 40 per cent faster than conventional trains, is, in today's jargon, "just around the corner".

What, one wonders, lies beyond that?

The shape of trains to come .... the Experimental Advanced Passenger Train (APT–E) was powered by gas turbines and pioneered the tilting body concept. When rounding curves at high speed the tilting mechanism gives passengers a smoother ride and automatically levels the coach body on reaching the straight.

# Check your speed

When you're on an Inter-City 125 train you'll probably find it hard to believe that you're actually travelling at 125 m.p.h.

But you can check for yourself by keeping an eye on the lineside distance posts, noting the time it takes to travel three-quarters of a mile, and relating to the speed table below.

SPEED TABLE

| Time taken to cover ¾ mile in seconds | 20 | 21 | 22 | 23 | 24 | 25 | 26 | 27 | 28 | 29 | 30 | 31 | 32 | 33 | 34 | 35 |
|---|---|---|---|---|---|---|---|---|---|---|---|---|---|---|---|---|
| Average speed in m.p.h. | 135 | 128 | 122 | 117 | 112 | 108 | 103 | 100 | 96 | 93 | 90 | 87 | 84 | 81 | 79 | 77 |

Or if you have a stop-watch you can get even more accurate results by applying the following formula.

$$\frac{3600}{\text{time in seconds between mile posts}} = \text{Speed in m.p.h.}$$

# Photographic acknowledgements . . .

National Railway Museum — Pages 3, 4 (Sturrock and loco),
5 (T.W. Worsdell), 6 (Worsdell, Ivatt),
8 (Thompson, Peppercorn),
10 (poster), 18 (map),
20/21 (props), 24, 25

P.W.B. Semmens — Page 8 (locos)

S.L. Rankin — Pages 14 (book), 28 (bottom left)

Fox Photos — Pages 26, 29 (bottom right)

H. Gordon Tidy — Pages 28–29 (overall)

Glasgow Bulletin — Pages 30, 31

J.H. Cooper-Smith — Pages 47, 62

Rodney Wildsmith — Pages 54, 55, 64

I.P.C. Publications Ltd. — Pages 90–91

The remainder of photographs and plans from British Rail photographic records.